Paper Clips Don't Grow on Trees

Add Value Not Cost to your Bottom Line

Catherine DeVrye

16
EasyRead Large

RHYW

Copyright Page from the Original Book

Woodslane Press Pty Ltd
7/5 Vuko Place, Warriewood, NSW 2102
Email: info@woodslane.com.au
Website: www.woodslane.com.au

Print edition first published by Woodslane Press in 2010
Ebook edition published by Woodslane Press in 2011

National Library of Australia Cataloguing-in-Publication entry

Author:	DeVrye, Catherine.
Title:	Paper clips don't grow on trees (electronic resource) : add value not cost to your bottom line / Catherine DeVrye.
Edition:	1st ed.
ISBN:	9781921874093 (ebook)
Subjects:	Small business—Management. Success in business. Business cycles.
Dewey Number:	658.041

Design and layout by Jenny Cowan Design

Set in 16 pt. Verdana

TABLE OF CONTENTS

Also by Catherine DeVrye

Who Says I Can't?/Serendipity Road-a memoir

Hope Happens! ... words of encouragement for tough times

Hot Lemon & Honey: Reflections for Success in Times of Change

The Customer Service Zoo-Create Customers for Life and a Life for Yourself

Good Service is Good Business-7 Simple Strategies for Success

Japan: An A-Z Guide of Living & Working in Japan

Sports Marketing & Promotion

Dedication

To my Scottish grandpa-David Smart

Smart by name and smart by nature

Caring of heart but careful with pennies

1

Introduction: fret or focus forward

'Despite the increase in the cost of living, the demand for it continues.' F Pegg

Concern about the economy is at the core of countless conversations in the world today. There is widespread worry from London to Los Angeles, Toronto to Tokyo, Durban to Dubai, Mumbai to Munich, Shanghai to Sydney. The latter is my home but during discussions with clients in those other cities, there seems a heightened sense of disquiet among small, medium and large organisations, alike.

In this increasingly global economy, none of us are immune from fluctuations in international financial markets. That much was evident during the infamous GFC (Global Financial Crisis) that gained momentum in 2008. expert opinion still varies on whether that is now behind us – or could ever occur again? It was, and maybe still is, all too easy to throw up our hands in despair with cries of:

'But, what can we do?'

'The ubiquitous 'they' should do something!' and, regardless of our political persuasion, of course 'The government should "fix" things'. All seem sound enough arguments in one aspect but totally worthless in another.

Crikey! All this negativity. I was admittedly sometimes swamped by it all, myself. What could I do to alter the economic climate? Frankly, not a damn thing! But what I *could* do was to critically re-visit my own business practices, consult with others and pen some pertinent points to help individuals and organisations feel more empowered. It's not necessary to simply adopt a 'slash and burn' approach to budgets but rather, to take positive steps to look at what *can* be done with finite resources. Rather than simply feel trapped in a hopeless situation, there might be gold in that dirt.

Fret or focus forward? This is always a choice we have, whether in good or bad times.

After decades of growth, the developed world has not witnessed such an economic slide since the Great Depression. From Wall Street to Main Street, times are still troubled and many adults remain nervous about personal finances and job security. What, if anything, *can* be done by the average man or woman in the workforce?

I believe it was President Franklin Roosevelt who said: 'We cannot protect the value of the dollar by passing the buck.' The good news is that tough times offer a greater incentive to re-think our standard modus operandi. There's no better time to eliminate waste-and stimulate value.

I'm no fiscal guru, but I believe this book can provide a basic blueprint to help move out of the red. It doesn't pretend to be a panacea for profitability but contains practical suggestions about what can be done to add value – not simply cost – to everyday operations. I trust it will serve as a catalyst to prompt every employee to be more economically responsible and prudent (possibly through necessity in tough times) in order to gain both immediate – and much longer term – benefits for their organisation.

My working class parents lived through the Great Depression and frequently reminded me that we weren't wealthy. Mum would say 'Money doesn't grow on trees, dear.' As a youngster, I never did quite understand why it was called the 'great' depression. And, frankly, nor did I appreciate the other clichés that my folks espoused to justify why we couldn't afford some luxury (which of course, I always thought was a necessity). You probably heard the same sort of things from your parents or grandparents...

'Look after the pennies and the pounds take care of themselves.'

'A penny saved is a penny earned.'

These days, a penny saved is ... shrapnel! (Unless you happen to be a rare coin collector!) But, even with no pennies in our currency system, it's still possible to save the equivalent of a cent to make a dollar.

Paper Clips Don't Grow on Trees contains practical examples of ways to cut costs without sacrificing quality. It suggests some positive, viable options to consider. even if just one *small* idea is implemented, it could make a *big* difference to any bottom line. It's important to point out that there is a real difference between being cost conscious and waste aware – or simply a cheapskate! Save where and when you can, so you have more to spend when and where you need to. Another age old adage of 'waste not – want not' is also consistent with today's growing environmental concerns.

I'm neither a die-hard environmentalist nor an economist-but a person who worked as an executive with IBM globally for a decade, a state government for nearly as long and briefly as CEO of a not-for-profit organisation. Now a small business owner for over 15 years, many assume my company name, CDV Management Pty Ltd, is derived from my own initials. This is partially so but those three little letters, prompted by my time at IBM represent – not just Catherine DeVrye – but **C**lients **D**eserve **V**alue.

This is what I've aimed to deliver; implementing lessons learned in large organisations, lessons learned through my own mistakes (the most costly!) and also those gleaned as a teacher, tour guide, waitress, dishwasher and cook. As an author who has spoken at conferences of leading organisations on five continents, I've also had the opportunity and privilege to gain first hand insight into what business practices have contributed to their success.

The concept for this book arose when a television station approached me for an interview to shed some light on the GFC. I initially declined and told the producer that I had absolutely no idea what was happening and was as nervous as the next person. However, she persuaded me that they weren't looking for an economist but wanted to discuss some principles contained in one of my earlier books, titled, *Hot Lemon and Honey: Reflections for Success in Times of Change.* These were indeed times of unprecedented change! So, I rather reluctantly did the interview. Below is a synopsis:

Q What should businesses do in this credit crisis?

A I'm not an economist and can't prescribe what businesses 'should' or 'shouldn't' do as every situation is unique. However, I do believe that every obstacle always presents some opportunity. Now may be an opportunity (in disguise) to assess the strengths and weaknesses of your overall business and the individual operational aspects within it.

Running a business is tough in the best of times but when things go well, it's easy to be complacent. Now is an opportunity to look at what you're doing well in terms of adding value to your customers, clients and stakeholders and keep focused on that! Get rid of anything else.

Q In an earlier book, you wrote that the seven most expensive words in any organisation were: 'We have always done it that way.' Is that still the case today?

A That was written nearly 10 years ago but remains at least as true today – maybe even more so. Just like we floss our teeth, we need brain floss to remove the build up of intellectual plaque over the years.

Q Does that mean that organisations need to adopt a radical new business model?

A Of course not. It's important not to throw out the baby with bath water but to assess what is – or is not – working. It's important to balance a 'stick with your knitting' strategy along with innovation.

But it's equally important to be brutally honest with what you need to do differently – or stop doing altogether.

Q So, should we be making across the board budget cuts?

A That's too much of a knee-jerk reaction. It's far better to take a more targeted approach; and there's no better time to take a good hard look at where money is wasted and how all your resources – capital and human – might be better employed.

We get bogged down in old patterns of behaviour when we're comfortable, and usually don't worry about paradigm shifts until forced to do so by some external force.

Q Are you saying this GFC could be a good thing?

A I've never seen anything like it in my lifetime and am not saying it's good at all. It's fuelled fears (not unjustifiable) of losing one's job, home or savings. But maybe – just maybe – there are opportunities that we can't imagine.

British philosopher, William Hazlitt, once wrote: 'Prosperity is a great teacher – adversity a greater one.'

That was over 300 years ago, but remains a timely reminder. I don't wish to sound like Pollyanna because I am, personally, extremely concerned. But I'm not going to waste energy on what I can't control – instead I'll choose to stay focused on what I can.

Q You make it sound so easy

A It's not easy at all. I'm as concerned as anyone because conference budgets are being cut, interest rates are uncertain; my bank has been taken over; and exchange rates seem to fluctuate like yo-yos when I commit to speak at an overseas conference.

At times like these, I remind myself that things work out best for the people who make the best of the way things work out. I then approach every 'challenge' more calmly, because as I said – and it's worth emphasising – there

> *is little point expending precious energy worrying about what we can't change – we all need to use our finite energy to focus on what we can do in any given situation.*

The interview ended and I left the studio, well aware that it was easier to talk about than do!

But something had to be done, so I dedicated the next morning to looking at potential cost savings in my own business, and then sent an email to my client base, containing the transcript of the interview. Many asked if they could reproduce it in their news-letters. A few suggested that the essence of the interview become the basis of a book; which would be timely to be released at the height of the GFC.

I'd actually already started to collect a thick file of information long before, as a dis-taste for waste in organisations has been a pet peeve of mine for many years. I thought I could quickly get a book to market to capitalize on the media and public interest. However, it seemed more responsible to pause and more carefully consider the format so that, hopefully, this information will stand the test of time. I have no doubt that small and medium sized businesses will quickly identify ideas that can be readily implemented. It should also be of benefit to larger organisations in both the private and public sectors.

If only I could conceive a formula to encourage every employee in a big organisation to think like a small business owner, I'd make a fortune bottling it. And organisations would save a fortune implementing it! Sadly, there is no such elixir, magic wand or silver bullet, but every cloud does indeed have a silver lining and tough financial times can assist in re-thinking old strategies for a new paradigm of whether individuals and organisations are adding value – or simply cost – to each process.

Paperclips Don't Grow on Trees has no quick fixes. It does not attempt to prescribe what individuals and individual businesses should or shouldn't do – because each situation is unique. It is not an economic essay, management manifesto or text book. It's more descriptive than prescriptive. It is intended to be an easily digestible book containing real life examples along with simple, timely and timeless tips to help individuals help themselves and their organisation – not just survive during troubled financial times but to thrive over the much longer term.

Pages contain a stand-alone idea, paragraph or mini essay to act as a thought starter. I don't expect that you'll agree with every thought as circumstances vary from industry to industry, region to region, case by case. Some examples may even appear somewhat contradictory. Not every concept will work for you but I guarantee that you'll get at least one cost saving idea that will more than recover your small investment in this book.

Read each chapter carefully – preferably with a pen in hand to write down your ***own*** ideas specific to your organisation. As you do so, start to form a habit; to routinely and repeatedly ask one simple question.

Ask this question with every purchase, with every hiring decision, with every allocation of time or resource ... Does this add value or cost? Value or cost to my business? Value or cost to my life? Value or cost to the life of another?

Let us get started.

2

Lettuce – let us help your bottom line

I've worked in government, big business with IBM, and now run a small, indeed micro, business as an author and speaker. Over the years, I've learned that whether large or small, there are only two ways to boost the bottom line—increase revenue or decrease expense. Sometimes, there is little you can do to increase revenue so there's a need to refocus on needless expense. I'm not talking about the slash and burn of staff but involving all staff in offering potential solutions.

For example, an airline made huge savings as a result of a suggestion from a new flight attendant. While clearing passenger meal trays into big plastic garbage bags, he noticed that most passengers didn't eat their lettuce and suggested the airline get rid of that garnish on the trays. Initially, this met with resistance from the executive chefs but as the airline was trying to encourage employee participation, they implemented a three month trial to remove the garnish, thinking it might only save a few hundred dollars but that they'd humour the employee who made the suggestion.

When they received no complaints from passengers, they stopped the lettuce completely and during one year, were amazed to learn that this resulted in savings of over $1.5 million!

Was the lettuce adding value or cost to the flying experience? Obviously, only cost. What is the equivalent of 'lettuce' in your organisation? What are you doing that you've always done that adds cost – not true value – to your customers?

Apologies to the lettuce farmers of this world – but it's not all gloom and doom for them if you think about how lettuce is now sold. You can buy a head of lettuce – organic or otherwise – in a supermarket or your local market. But you can also just buy a handful of lettuce leaves, already pre washed.

Yes, it costs more to buy in this manner but many consumers are more time sensitive than cost sensitive, so those who sell lettuce in small, already clean quantities, with no wastage, add value to many time-poor consumers. It could be argued that they are also adding cost (to both consumers and the environment) in terms of whatever extra packaging they use. However, the point is that they are adding value by giving a choice to that consumer who is happy to pay a bit more.

Again, I ask you to pause and reflect: 'What is the equivalent of your lettuce?'

3

Fair for fare

In 1987 American Airlines saved $40,000 by eliminating one olive – just one – from each salad served in first class.

With budget airlines these days, you'll likely receive no food at all. That's fair enough since the fare is accordingly reduced in alignment with lower customer expectations, and passengers are aware in advance that they need to bring their own food or purchase it separately on board.

Some airlines advertise that celebrity chefs design their gourmet fare but if you don't pay a first or business class fare, few travellers expect a first class meal.

I've noticed that some carriers, rather than give a standard amenity kit to passengers, now offer a selection of toothbrushes and toiletries from a trolley.

Expand that earlier question: What's the equivalent of your lettuce-or olive-or?

4

Don't throw in the towel

Think laterally and make sure that whatever you do is aligned with the values of your organisation and the expectations of your market place.

In most hotels around the globe, there are now usually signs in the bathroom, encouraging guests along the lines: 'We are committed to protecting the environment and by reusing your towel; it will save on water usage'. At the risk of being cynical, I doubt that the environment is the key reason that most hotels ask guests to reuse towels and suspect it may have more to do with economic than eco-friendly reasons. However, let's face it – most of us don't have fresh towels at home every day.

Some hotels are now extending the reuse of towels to the reuse of sheets – and have a similar tent card on your bed to give you the option of not having your sheets changed daily.

It would likely be a greater incentive if hotels offered a slight reduction on your bill if you chose not to have your room serviced every day.

I predict that it will only be a matter of time before this becomes the norm. After all, the suggestion to reuse towels, now fairly standard around the world, apparently started in a small way in a remote area of Tasmania many years ago. During the protests relating to the damming of the Franklin River, it's alleged that an accommodation operator near this remote wilderness area became one of the first (if not the first) to suggest guests reuse their towels. At the time, this was somewhat unheard of but because eco tourism was in its early stages and most visitors to that area were environmentally sensitive of the need to preserve water, it wasn't a big ask to reuse a towel. This was aligned with the values of the hotel as well as the core value systems of most guests. They still had the choice to receive a clean towel every day but possibly felt a little guilty doing so in that location at the height of the debate on the dam. It's now common practice to give guests the choice to hang up their towel or throw it in the tub for a fresh one.

To many hotels, the clean towels daily were the equivalent of their 'lettuce' – adding cost, not value to most customers. Don't throw in the towel in regard to cost savings but again, pause and reflect on the equivalent of your lettuce. And, if we're always clean after a shower, in theory, maybe we should never need to wash towels (but let's not go there).

5

Eco-friendly is eco-nomic

Of course, you knew that-didn't you?

Let's be frank. Most businesses don't simply implement better environmental practices because they want to be a do-gooder but because doing good for the environment will help boost their bottom line.

Don't just take my word for it. Here's a short excerpt from the 2007 Harvard Business Review in an article by Charles Lockwood, titled 'Building the Green Way':

'Just five or six years ago, the term "green building" evoked visions of tie-dyed, granola-munching denizens walking around barefoot on straw mats as wind chimes dangled near open windows. Today the term suggests lower overhead costs, greater employee productivity, less absenteeism and stronger employee attraction and retention ... green is not simply getting respect; it is rapidly becoming a necessity.'

He goes on to claim that green buildings can also boost employee productivity up to 15% because they use materials that don't emit toxins.

The Qantas in flight magazine of February 2010 announced awards for excellence in sustainable tourism; consideration was given to more than just the buzz words of being 'green' or 'carbon neutral'.

It is not the intent of this book to explore those obviously important aspects – although the book is indeed printed on recycled paper. What was relevant about these awards in the context of value and cost were that many of the initiatives being introduced that reduced cost without reducing value to the client.

The South Australian winner was the Hilton Hotel in Adelaide, which had impressive major reductions in water, gas and electricity use despite an increase in hotel numbers. They engaged guests by donating five dollars to Trees for Life every time a room was not serviced. It's a great initiative but I suspect that if they also offered a five dollar reduction to the actual guest, they'd have even further savings on servicing fewer rooms each day. Hilton also recycled food with a local shelter and sourced 97% of the hotel's produce from South Australia.

The Victorian winner was the Alto Hotel, which used 100% wind-generated electricity and rainwater for some cisterns, gardening and cleaning. They eliminated plastic bottles for toiletries and promoted seasonal foods. Yes, all of this makes them a good corporate citizen but also boosts their bottom line long-term. The article goes on to quote one of Alto's directors, who claims occupancy has been in excess of 90% during the height of the Global Financial Crisis, and that their fastest growth market is in corporate and government organisations with 'green procurement' policies; closely followed by environmentally-conscious European leisure travellers.

Many hotels have now replaced small bottles of shampoo and lotions with dispensers; saving money and reducing waste. One establishment apparently saved nearly $370,000 per year after installing dispensers at a cost of $91,000

Eco-friendly makes long-term eco-nomic sense. As someone who invested a considerable amount of money building an eco-friendly home, my motive was not just philosophical to contribute in a small way to save the planet but to ultimately save on costs when I become a pensioner on a fixed income!

6

Renew on a shoestring

An interior designer friend has over 20 years of experience as a consultant to a five star international hotel chain and says that, on average, most hotel rooms are re-furbished every five to eight years; depending on wear and tear and readily available funds.

However, if budgets are tight, this average time frame of a major renovation can usually be extended by a couple of years. Rather than costly replacement of carpet, bathroom tiles and furniture, it's often possible to make some lower cost cosmetic changes to still give a fresh appearance.

For example, the simple switch from an old television to a flat screen unit was a relatively low cost expenditure but gave the immediate perception of a more modern room in 2010. This, combined with replacing conventional bedspreads with trendier duvets in the hippest colour was much less costly than a total renovation but still gave that crisp, modern feel at a fraction of the cost when a weary traveller first walked through the door.

Likewise, the hotel extended the lifetime of their fine linen table cloths in their upmarket restaurant, by simply placing white butchers paper at a diagonal angle over most of the table. This resulted in fewer permanent stains on the linen, plus the added advantage that the paper could be more quickly replaced with each setting, yet still look classy enough for their fine dining restaurant.

7

Office furniture

Instead of rushing out to buy new office furniture and equipment, great savings can be found if you know where to look.

If you need to purchase office furniture or appliances, check out auctions (live or online) or discount office furniture warehouses.

Personally, I'd be happy to buy a second hand filing cabinet or book shelf in good clean condition. I would, however, be reluctant to purchase second hand electronics, which could easily be a false economy of scale if they were no longer under warranty.

8

Where does that money go?

Do you really know what your actual expenses are? Do they vary greatly from year to year; month to month or by season? It's amazing how many businesses, especially smaller ones, have no idea of their costs, which may result in a knee-jerk reaction to cut spending in the wrong areas if times are tough.

It's seems blatantly obvious advice, but keep track of all expenses. Make a list and budget in advance (although there are always unexpected expenses). Check out areas where you could cut down and save money *without* sacrificing performance or customer satisfaction.

9

Take the blinkers off before you need to

Do you have blinds spots? Are vulnerabilities only visible in tough times. Take your blinkers off before you need to.

John Caslione and Philip Kotler of the Kellogg School of Management write in *Chaotics* (Amacom, 2008):

'Executives should strive to make their operations more efficient and to reduce unproductive expenditures, especially in areas that show signs of bloat – regardless of the business conditions. Let's be honest: Discipline tends to slip during a lengthy upturn in the economy.'

They go on to encourage management to keep an eye on the ball in order to be in a position to continue with growth once the market picks up. They also suggest this is unlikely if management succumbs to across board cuts. It's far better to take focused and measured actions.

Some CEOs may ask each branch office to cut expenses by a certain percentage – but each branch manager can still make the decision on what actually gets cut. This makes sense since each branch faces different threats and opportunities in their unique markets with varying customer expectations.

Be sure to preserve areas that customers value most. How do you find out what they most value?

Ask them. Full stop!

10

Share the word for true value to share holders

In what might be dubbed a 'lettuce' litmus learning test, let us give another example of adding cost – not value...

I'm a modest shareholder in a few public companies. Each year, they would send full-colour, glossy annual reports, which I seldom ever read (as I'm one of those boring investors who buys blue chip stock and puts it in the bottom drawer). I'd read my dividend statement but throw the rest of the report in the bin. I knew it was an expensive document but also knew it was largely a public relations exercise and I didn't have time to read their spin.

Not only did the annual report cost a lot to produce and print but the cost of postage would have also detracted from the bottom line of my returns. So, many years ago, I suggested to a couple of companies (in which I had a particular interest, as they were also clients) that they give shareholders the option of receiving the annual report or opting out. I never did receive any feedback on that suggestion but a number of years later I noticed that most companies were beginning to give shareholders the choice to opt out of the glossy publication.

This was before the days of email, so that's now another option for those who would like to receive the information – but not necessarily favour killing forests to produce a glossy brochure. The same holds true for paperless brokerage statements. Of course, companies still have sunk production costs, plus some added web development costs but the real savings lie in distribution. And since I've already offended the lettuce farmers of the world, let me make it clear to the printing industry that there are indeed times when a glossy brochure adds greater value – perceived or otherwise – to a product or service.

I'd love the companies to quantify the cost savings to them when shareholders opted *out* of receiving the report. Such savings would likely be more if they had to opt *in* to receive the glossy section of it. There are, of course, compliance issues in regard to basic information which shareholders must receive but that can still be provided in black and white.

11

Email, snail mail or no mail

Likewise, there's no need to send via post most rental or bank statements; or write and mail cheques when funds can be transferred electronically. However, please remember that not all of your customers have access to computers. I don't mean to stereotype, as my 87 year-old uncle is very tech savvy, but many elderly people are not and have no wish to learn.

Is it best to send email, sea mail, airmail or courier? Does it need an envelope, bubble wrap or a box?

Does it absolutely need to be there by a certain time? Or is the delivery date not time-critical?

Many years ago, I had a secretary who couriered every book ordered. I wasn't aware of this until receipt of the monthly invoice from the courier company that was about 10 times higher than normal. The cost of the courier far exceeded any profit made on the books.

Her logic was that because the book was on customer service, they should receive it immediately. I had overlooked explaining the cost reality and that people generally expect delivery of a book within a few days; whereas if it's a life-saving medical supply, there's obviously more urgency.

We then reviewed whether books needed to be in an envelope, bubble wrap or box-and it was quickly determined that while it depended on the size of book and number of books, an envelope was generally adequate.

I explained that I was also paying for her time so I didn't want her to spend half an hour to save a dollar. However, if in doubt during my many absences from the office, she should always try to imagine that every cent she spent was coming out of her own pocket-so if she thought any expense was justified, that it would probably be OK by me.

Much to her delight, she later discovered that in some instances, it was cheaper to use a courier for delivery of a box of books to some locations; but she never again sent an individual book via courier.

To save time waiting in queues at the post office, we now have a list of the costs of posting individual books, CDs and DVDs – so no need to visit the post office for any standard orders. And as e-books and podcasts become more popular, trips to the post office may be further reduced (although I must confess I hope and believe that the hard copy book will be around for a long time to come).

A secretary with one of my large international clients could not quite grasp the concept of added cost. They bought over 1,500 copies of one of my books for every delegate attending their overseas conference at which I was speaking. I strongly suggested that they place the order a couple of months in advance where the freight costs would have added approximately 40 cents to the cost of each book-but – because she left it until the last moment – it cost nearly 10 times that amount to air freight the books to Hong Kong. (This certainly didn't add any value to the book or to the delegates!) At the time, her company was going through a boom time and seemed to have unlimited budgets – but only a couple of years later, was it any wonder they were struggling financially?

Encourage every employee to think of it as their business (easier said than done!) and to always ask the question: 'What would I do if this was my business – if I bore every cost?'

12

Would you like fries with that?

Apart from cleanliness, there is nothing more important than the food outlet meeting your expectations of the meal – whether that be an elegant fine dining experience or a quick takeaway.

Let's look at the difference between value and cost at a five star hotel and a MacDonald's. Which is best? Well, it depends...

You certainly wouldn't expect to go to a five star hotel and have the waiter in a baseball cap ask: 'Would you like fries with that?'

But, can you imagine walking into MacDonald's one day and being greeted by a maitre de in a tuxedo. He shows you to your table with a white linen tablecloth, sparkling cutlery and crystal, floral arrangement and violinist playing in the background.

Would that exceed your expectations of Macca's? Of course. Until about the third bite of your Big Mac when you think to yourself ... 'Hold on, this is costing more money and taking more time.'

All around the world, MacDonald's has set expectations of low cost, fast food, so by adding all those glamorous extras, does that really add value or cost to your MacDonald's experience? It's probably just cost.

A number of years ago, when a few friends and I cycled over the Andes, we went into a fast food pizza outlet in Buenos Aires for a 'carbohydrate loading' and much to our surprise, there were white linen table cloths. That apparently was the minimum standard for any sort of dining in Argentina at the time (at least it was before their economic crisis in 2001).

I also remember visiting a MacDonald's near Wall Street in new York that had a grand piano automatically playing and floral arrangement during the lunch hour ... it was thought that this added value to reduce the stress for some brokers.

Whether you love 'em or hate 'em, you must concede that MacDonald's maintains an enviable consistency of food, cleanliness and air conditioning. Although I admittedly don't eat there all that often, I'm a fan because I know what I'm going to get. A few years ago, the concierge at the up market Versace Hotel on the Gold Coast had a look of horror on his face as I passed through the lobby to my room with a Macca's bag in hand from their outlet next door. I was just too tired and rushed to sit down and have an elaborate meal and wasn't sure how long room service would take. I'd have quite happily paid Versace prices for my humble Macdonald's fries that evening because that's all I wanted at the time – it had nothing to do with cost. And yes, I did linger over a sumptuous Versace meal the following night.

13

Nothing fishy about listening to customers – and staff

In another instance, a grocery store increased fish sales by listening to a junior employee who had first listened to a customer. The story goes something like this...

Each week, about 10 different women were invited into the conference room at the grocery store in return for a shopping voucher. They were asked a series of questions by a market researcher about one particular aspect of the store. Staff members responsible for that particular section were also present.

On a particular day, when the focus was on the fish department, feedback was generally positive. However, one of the women commented that although the fish seemed to be of high quality, it would be better if it were fresh. The manager defensively assured her that it was indeed fresh. It was trucked from the sea every morning, hygienically wrapped in plastic, put in refrigerated stainless steel containers and any unsold fish was given to a charity at the end of the day. A young employee, who hadn't worked there long, kept quiet during the customer focus group but later suggested that they might want to attempt to modify the incorrect perception that this woman had. To his credit, the manager of the fish department agreed to an experiment whereby the next day they wrapped half the fish as always and simply spread the other half on freshly crushed ice.

As predicted, the fish on the ice sold more than the packaged product, even though it was exactly the same fish! What's more, there were additional savings on the labour and the packaging, as the packaging was not only perceived as not adding value, but was in fact perceived as distracting from the value of 'fresh' fish. The woman was absolutely wrong in her assumption that the fish wasn't fresh-but her perception was absolutely correct.

By listening with an open mind, the manager's decision to dispose of the packaging was not only good for the company, but good for the environment.

Get everyone involved in solutions to make sure that you and they add value – not cost!

14

Good things come in small packages

That's another of my mother's maxims. It's amazing how much I find myself agreeing with her these days, when I once rejected most of her advice!

A large proportion of the cost of consumer items to us – and the environment – is tied up in excessive packaging. Whenever I un-wrap my duty free purchases to fit into carry-on luggage, it never ceases to amaze me that a tiny bottle of perfume or skin care lotion is buried deep within a large, impressive looking box. It's hard to tell from the display how much perfume is really inside that big bottle, which itself is inside that even bigger box that I immediately discard.

However, it's equally hard to dismiss the marketing appeal of such packaging, especially if bought as a gift. After all, presentation of a present is almost as important as the gift itself.

So, it's worth questioning whether your products warrant (often wasteful) packaging. Sometimes it adds value (or at least, perceived value). Sometimes it does not.

Think also about packaging used internally within your organisation. The story is told of a multi-millionaire businessman who chastises staff and suppliers if they present him with an elaborately bound proposal. 'Cut the crap – I just want the bare bones facts,' he bellowed one day. They soon got the idea. Yet, strong visuals and presentation do indeed add significant value to many of our buying decisions – just ask the folks in advertising and brand awareness. Again, it all depends...

When I was about to sell an eco-friendly home, I interviewed prospective realtors who had been recommended and was particularly impressed by two. Both seemed ethical, offered realistic market price expectations, proposed a similar advertising campaign, had a good track record of sales in the neighbourhood and seemed equally customer focused. And yes, they had the same commission structure.

I also liked them both as individual sales people, so who should I chose? In the end, it came down to a gut feel but I can't help but think I was possibly influenced by the glossy packaging of the proposals – that is, influenced in a negative sense by one. Since I was selling an up market, eco-friendly home, I recognised that it was important to portray an impression of style and elegance – yet one proposal was wrapped in expensive packaging that seemed to not so much advertise my house as it did promote the realtor. More importantly, any 'over the top' packaging of materials was not aligned with my values; nor likely aligned with the value system of a buyer wanting to purchase an eco-friendly home!

I truly didn't need – nor did I appreciate – their packaging. Likewise, with postage, we seldom need to put an envelope in a box within a shipping box or an envelope inside another envelope.

If sending non-confidential materials to multiple individuals at one company at the same address, you can often include everything in one envelope – paying only one lot of postage – as usually someone in the mail room opens the mail anyway and discards the envelope.

By all means, make sure your goods are adequately protected during handling and transport but be careful that any excessive and expensive packaging doesn't send your customers packing.

15

Time is money – but money is also money

Most of us are time-poor, so anything you can do to free up time for colleagues, customers or bosses will be seen by them as true added value.

Remember to factor in the cost of your time as well. Whether your charge out rate is $50 or $500 per hour, do you want to spend $100 or $1,000 worth of your time trying to save $50? The answer to that question may depend on how much free time you have, how tight your cash flow is or how much tax you pay.

Let's say you earn $100 an hour and pay 50% tax. If you spend two hours on a standard task that you might otherwise pay someone else $15 per hour to do, it doesn't make a lot of sense. Do not undervalue your own time – it is the most important asset we have. Time is money, but money is also money. If you have the time, it may be best to do something yourself, but if you're already working 10-12 hour days, it may be a worthwhile investment to employ someone else.

I know a well-respected consultant who spends five to 10 minutes to steam an unused 55 cent stamp off an envelope! He's been accused of having deep pockets and being ridiculously tight with money. Maybe so – but always better to be neat and tidy than tight and needy. Yes, he is meticulous (some would say anal) and this does not seem an efficient use of time for someone who charges $450 per hour in consulting fees.

However, that's his choice; and how you allocate resources is most always your choice The important thing to remember is to simply always ask the question: Is this a good use of my time – right now – given these circumstances?

As the late management guru, Peter Drucker, stated: 'There is nothing so senseless as doing efficiently that which need not be done at all.'

16

Grant or grunt

The CEO of an NGO (Non Government Organisation) told me that much of their funding-comes from various grants. Those for which they are eligible are advertised in various professional journals. They tend to re-apply to their traditional funding sources but occasionally they will spot other potential forms of revenue. Recently, one of her staff applied for a grant worth $3,000 and was successful in her bid.

The CEO was less than impressed. 'Why weren't you happy?' I asked, thinking that the employee would have been surprised that the CEO was not pleased with the result.

'Well, it was a 22 page application that had to be submitted in triplicate and probably killed countless trees with the various drafts it went through. But, much more importantly, we estimate that it used much more than $3,000 in time spent to collate all the information! That time would have been better spent on delivering core services to our stakeholders.' So in the end it was a lot of organisational grunt for very little grant money.

Her logic was hard to fault as she went on to say that she subsequently implemented a policy that staff members could only use organisational time to apply for grants worth more than $20,000 – which would yield a reasonable return on their investment of time.

This was an excellent example of how many employees, however well meaning, place no monetary value on their time. This is especially true in larger government or not-for-profit organisations and quite a contrast to the opposite end of the continuum where lawyers bill out every eight minute block (or portion thereof). I've also heard stories that some even charge if you send a simple 'thanks' reply to an email ... but that's another issue.

17

You be the judge – is cost cutting always wise?

Speaking of things legal, another mutual friend, a judge, overheard this conversation and confirmed:

'Yes, some lawyers do overcharge for their time but most simply charge for their actual time, which is fair enough. But let me tell you the other side of the coin and how short sighted some courts are in their supposed cost cutting measures, which result in lawyers and judges wasting time.'

She went on to outline that there had been recent measures to cut costs in regional courts, which entailed substantial reductions in, and sometimes elimination of, administrative staff. Yes, it may have cut bottom line costs in terms of that individual's actual salary, but it resulted in much more highly paid judges having to carry out those basic administrative tasks, creating longer delays. So rather than hearing, for example, 10 cases a day, they may have only heard seven (a 30% reduction in their output), and as they also had to play a greater role in the transition of clearing the court of one case in order to hear another, this resulted in additional delays for lawyers from all parties. Of course it was only fair that the lawyers be compensated for their time, but it was the end client who paid for this.

'I estimate the so-called cost savings of a $40,000 per year administrative person 'costs' the system at least three times that amount.'

You be the judge if that cost cutting measure was a smart move. Certainly, the bottom line may look marginally better but any quantitative measure of the number of cases heard per hours spent would probably look substantially worse from an efficiency standpoint.

Generally speaking, if you could otherwise be doing something worth $100 per hour, it's probably better to outsource more mundane tasks and pay others $20 per hour - but only if it adds value at that point in time.

Another friend cited a similar occurrence in the academic world and complained that, as a professor, she now spent a disproportionate amount of time on administrative work following recent staff cuts. However, when pushed, she admitted that the administrator had never really been fully utilised by the teaching staff. In this instance, rather than eliminate the position entirely, it probably made more sense to switch the role from full time to part time.

Circumstances change, so it's important to re-evaluate from time to time. Let me provide another example...

Like many small businesses, I started as a sole operator and later employed a full time personal assistant. This model worked well for many years until at one stage, it seemed that I spent a disproportionate amount of time trying to actually generate enough work to keep her busy with administrative tasks, rather than focusing on my core creative business of writing books and crafting presentations. I rather reluctantly suggested that her hours be reduced – I didn't want to lose her and assumed she needed the full time income. Much to my delight, she was more than happy to work part time as she wanted to spend more time with her elderly mother. I cut costs and got more value from the days she worked.

To outsource or not to outsource? That is the question. It's a question for which there is no blanket answer. It may well be worthwhile to outsource knowledge and expertise but be very careful before you outsource your touch points with customers. It's a vital link in the value chain and you may be surprised to learn that many organisations which once outsourced call centres overseas, where wages were lower, have since brought them back to their local country.

Again, it's important to always consider both sides of the value/cost coin.

18

You can quote me on that

Do you ever feel that some suppliers take your loyalty for granted and make no effort to offer a competitive price? Or are you like me and seldom bother to shop around?

If I've been happy with a good or service, I am reluctant to change – even for a slightly lower price. Research will back up that if you are perceived as a good service provider, you can charge 9-10% more for the same basic good or service.

An acquaintance constantly monitors interest rates in the paper and frequently refinances his business and home loans if he can get even a 0.1% difference elsewhere. I honestly don't know how much he saves in the long run in terms of exit fees and his time.

With the constant changes in fee structures of banks and telecommunications companies, it seems they are always offering a better deal and a better package if you sign up for 12 or 24 months. No sooner are you locked into that package, than your previous provider comes up with yet a better deal! Well, maybe not quite that drastic – and I can't see the point of a small business monitoring minor increases on a daily or weekly basis – but again, if you're a large company with millions of transactions, the most minor difference in fees soon accumulates.

On the other hand, I'm sure Choice magazine would advise that someone like me be much more vigilant. Only recently, a young friend urged me to change phone providers. I was reluctant to do so as past experience has taught me that this can be fraught with pitfalls. However, I found out the 'deal' from the alternative provider and then called my existing provider, mentioning that I was likely to leave if they could not match the other offer. Sure enough, they reduced my phone bill by $22 a month and internet service by $30 per month though some sort of bundling. Yes, it took nearly an hour to do but hey, that's $624 a year in my pocket instead of theirs.

If you offer customers a credit card facility, look at what you pay the bank for merchant fees. It obviously depends on volume and comes as no surprise that big retailers are offered lower rates than a local shop. But there may be better rates available if you're a member of a local chamber of commerce or trade association, who has negotiated better rates for members on your behalf.

It may also be possible to simply ask. One relatively small business associate, who paid 2.2% on every credit card transaction, approached his bank with an offer that he received from one of their competitors. His bank matched that offer and he now only pays 0.9% per transaction, saving over $20,000 a year. You can't always bank on such savings but you've got no hope if you never ask the question.

19

Ask and ye shall receive – sometimes

In the night market of Shanghai or the Grand Bazaar of Istanbul – and many other parts of the world – bargaining is the norm. Only the most naïve customers would readily pay the first price quoted by the vendors. It's almost a game to bargain in these locations (although I've been mildly annoyed with friends who haggle with a poor shop owner over a few cents by our Western standards; which would be substantially more appreciated by a merchant in an emerging nation who has an extended family to feed).

I'm not much of a negotiator at the best of times, but as a tourist I try my best to play the game in a good spirited fashion. There have even been times when I've successfully negotiated a lower price for some souvenir – but then given the proprietor more than agreed, as I still thought it was a bargain and liked them and/or their story.

I easily ask for a discount if I'm buying six pashminas as presents in Mumbai but had never even considered requesting a discount for bulk buys in Sydney, London or Chicago – and certainly not on any goods or services related to my business.

'Silly you!' says a friend's husband. He is in charge of purchasing for a large organisation and obviously has more buying power and clout than a small business. But he encourages his mates in owner-operated businesses to always ask suppliers for a discount. There are savings to be had if you buy in bulk, pay cash or even negotiate a discount for prompt payment.

As I was about to reprint an earlier book (no longer in print from the original publisher), he encouraged me to ask the printer for a 20 cent discount on each book that cost over five dollars to print. It seemed somewhat penny pinching for a mere 20 cents but as he pointed out: 'Sure, you only save 20 cents per book but if you print 3,000 copies, that will deliver $600 immediately to your bottom line.' I tentatively asked the printer and much to my surprise, he agreed without batting an eyelid!

As my buyer friend pointed out, it may not always work but it seldom offends. Most sellers know their workable margins so what does it cost to ask?

Ironically, I was in the process of writing this book at the time and couldn't believe that in over 15 years of small business I'd never asked a supplier to revisit their quoted price. Silly me, indeed!

I really should be more assertive and vigilant to practice what I'm now preaching in terms of reducing cost without reducing value; and more frequently ask suppliers to sharpen their pencils – while still maintaining a good relationship that both parties find profitable.

I've only been game enough to try it on a couple of occasions since; once the price of the unit was fixed but the salesperson then offered free delivery (valued at $90). Ask and ye shall receive – sometimes. no cost but potential savings.

On the other hand, if you're a supplier, don't give away any more than you need to. A friend purchased taps from a plumbing supply shop and as he reached for his wallet, simply commented in passing that they 'seemed rather expensive'. He had every intention of paying full price but just as he was taking out his credit card the cashier replied: 'No worries mate-we'll take 10% off.' The customer was initially pleased but then began to wonder if the margins were ridiculously high in the first place.

20

Horses for courses

In spite of my earlier comments about cutting back on glossy annual reports, I get a fair bit of printing done and have learned that different printers have different specialist equipment which makes some more efficient (and lower cost) at printing large full colour formats and others much better at black and white A4 copies.

Once I have all the art work (which is always an additional cost) with one printer – and they have the correct colour tones etc. – I am reluctant to change. However, in one instance I needed an urgent rush job which my normal local printer couldn't accommodate, so I had no choice but to drive 10 kilometres to another outlet.

I was sure it would not only take more of my time to drive, park, wait but that it would cost more since they didn't have the original artwork. Much to my surprise (and thanks to the digital age) they were able to do it immediately and it was 40% less than my normal local printer. So is it best to maintain my loyalty with him and ask him to match the price in future? Or just go to the guy who gave me a better deal without even asking?

The truth of the matter is that it's not uncommon for your previous suppliers to become complacent about your business – obtaining the occasional quote on jobs that you have done regularly may indeed prove a great use of your time.

One size does not fit all. Look before you leap. Think before you spend.

21

Fax or fiction – do you really need that?

Businesses frequently receive calls from telecommunications companies asking them if they are happy with their phone provider and offering some new deal to switch suppliers. It could become a full time role to switch back and forth with the ensuing paperwork. However, just as most of us have an annual dental check, it is probably worth setting aside a fixed amount of time to have an annual equipment audit of your business.

How many phone lines do you need? Do you have enough or too many? In the electronic age of scanners, do you still need a dedicated fax line? Or a split line? Can you simply use your old machine to occasionally plug it in if you need to receive or send a fax?

A friend recently moved house and, in the course of waiting for the phone to be hooked up, realised that he didn't really need a dedicated home line since most people now contacted him on his mobile out of hours. He'd observed that 90% of incoming faxes were just advertising and that he seldom used his fax machine, so simply shifted his fax number to his home phone line (and made the ring tone silent), which still allows him to call out for the cost of a local call but saved him about $30 per month in line rental alone. That's $360 a year in after tax dollars.

Was it worth it in terms of time? In his case, absolutely, as he had to deal with the phone company anyway. 'I doubt I'd have bothered if I wasn't moving but only wish I'd done it a few years ago – I'd have saved enough for a new set of golf clubs.'

His young niece overheard part of this conversation and innocently asked: 'What's a fax?'

22

Fax off – faux pas

Prompted by my friend's account of savings on his fax line, a few months later I decided to do likewise. One minor glitch was that my internet broadband was connected to that fax line but both ADSL provider and phone company assured me that they could easily switch it to my phone line since they were in the same location and there would be no change to the configuration.

To cut a long story short (and believe me, there were many long stories – with countless calls to the phone company and ADSL supplier!) I am indeed now saving $30 per month. However, there was a $150 charge, plus four hours of employing an IT expert at $160 per hour to alter the configurations which 'should' have worked just fine with the 'simple' switch.

So according to my calculations, and assuming I keep the same service (which will almost certainly be superseded by wireless), it would take me the rest of my working life to recoup the $30 per month savings of switching – not to mention my own time and frustration over the 10 day period when I felt like telling the phone company and ADSL provider to fax off (as they both claimed it was the others' issue).

I seem to have particularly bad 'tech karma' with even the so-called simplest of changes. Possibly I killed a carrier pigeon in a previous life – so please be warned that not every seemingly obvious saving for someone else may necessarily be so for you.

The moral of this story is that all that glisters is not gold. Rather than take advantage of a tax concession to purchase a new laptop, I simply extended the guarantee on my 'old' one. Assuming it keeps going, it will then be three years 'old' and likely qualify as a museum relic. But it does everything I now require and if I take into account the need to format, update software and transfer all the data, there would probably be no savings whatsoever.

23

Perception is reality – how sweet it is

There's an old story about a young girl whose grandfather gave her pocket money to buy lollies at the local shop when she visited his small town. One day, when she arrived back at his house, she commented: 'It wasn't the nice lady today. It was the bad lady. She doesn't give me as much candy and takes candy away.' Her grandfather was puzzled because two sisters had run the shop for many years; both seemed pleasant and were well-respected in the town, so he doubted they would diddle his granddaughter. On her next visit, he accompanied her to the shop and as they walked in, she whispered, 'It's the bad lady.' Her grandfather urged her to just place her normal order of 250 grams and not say anything as he observed the scales.

The 'bad lady' seemed pleasant enough to him, as she scooped a pile of lollies onto the scale. It was approximately 300 grams, so she took a few out, still leaving the little girl with slightly more than the 250 grams she had ordered.

After they left the shop with a cheery good bye from the 'bad' lady, he queried his granddaughter as to why she thought the lady was 'bad'. 'Didn't you see grandpa? She put lollies in the scale and then ... she took them *out* again' his granddaughter stated indignantly.

He tried to explain that she did indeed give the little girl slightly more than what she had paid for but the youngster was adamant that the other lady in the shop was nicer.

A few days later, the grandfather noticed the 'nice' lady in the shop so went in to buy the same lollies. He astutely observed that she scooped a smaller amount of lollies into the scale and *then* added one at a time until the correct weight was reached. On the other hand, the 'bad' lady first put a lot in and then took some out. In fact, the 'bad' lady was even a bit more generous in her serving.

Both were equally pleasant but his granddaughter's perception saw the 'nice' lady always giving her more and the 'bad' lady taking some away. The perception of the child was totally incorrect in terms of the value that she received, but it was still reality in her own mind.

Do your customers have the right perception of the actual value you provide?

24

Don't just add on – add value

Let's take a quick look at a slightly different aspect of adding value – not cost. The surf culture seems the antithesis to the business one. Yet, surprisingly, there are lessons to be learned for those of us who spend considerably more time in blue suits than wet suits! In fact, we can learn from each other.

As an individual who didn't try the sport until I was on the 'wrong' side of 40, I had the dubious distinction of being the oldest person enrolled in the surf school. Call it a mid-life crisis, if you will, but it had been something which I'd always wanted to do and living on Australia's famous Manly beach meant I had no excuses not to try.

As it was an Australian winter (akin to a Canadian summer of my youth) my first stop was one of the many surf shops to buy a wet suit. not being a young, blonde and beautiful babe, I was totally ignored by the young sales assistant when I inquired about the wide range of wet suits available. When beckoned, he reluctantly came over and asked:

"Is it for your daughter?"

This did nothing to build customer rapport! I calmly informed him that it was for me so he simply pointed at a rack and I was none the wiser. As I walked out, I noticed a sign on the door that read:

'Our normal hours are 10am-5pm, but that's not always the case because we may be out surfing. If surf's up, we believe that surfing comes first and everything else comes second.'

So much for the customer coming first! It's a pity I didn't see that sign *before* I walked in.

I hesitantly walked into the next store – same layout, same products and spotted yet another salesman young enough to be my son. However, this young man had a totally different attitude from the guy in the last shop. He knew and explained his product, gave me some wetsuits to try on and was genuinely helpful. When I emerged from the fitting room to inquire if I had the right size, he thankfully didn't burst into fits of laughter and assured me it was OK.

By this time, he had acquired enough information to know that I wasn't familiar with the surf and was conscious of both warmth and safety. So, he suggested that I also purchase some flippers to give me more strength in the water, while I learned to body surf. He then asked:

'You don't want to lose them, do you?' An obvious question, I replied in the negative and found myself purchasing ankle straps. Anyone who has ever been in sales would recognise this as a classic technique called 'upselling' or 'add-ons'. As I was about to pay for these three purchases, he added:

"You look like a fun sort of lady and we've got a sale on boogie boards."

I laughed and replied:

'Thanks but I think these add-ons and upselling (of which he was a master) have gone too far.'

But guess who now owns a purple and yellow boogie board! Handing him my credit card, having spent a small fortune when I simply wanted to buy a wet suit, I jokingly asked:

'So, what else does a middle aged surfie chick need?'

With a huge smile, he replied; 'A middle aged surfie bloke.'

This stereotyped surf shop salesman, complete with long blonde hair in a ponytail, earring and dolphin tattoo, had personality plus. He was a marked contrast to his counterpart in the first shop. Both places had the same basic product and the sales staff looked the same, but the service was astonishingly different. As a person who had once been in sales with IBM, I recognised the technique but didn't for a moment feel that I was just 'up sold', but 'right sold'. As I walked out I felt – and til this day feel – that he had added value – not just cost – to my initial intent to purchase a single wetsuit.

About a year after I became more comfortable on the boogie board, I thought I'd try an actual surfboard and it doesn't take a rocket scientist to figure out that I returned to the second shop.

If only the salesman in the first shop (which went out of business) had been able to suspend his traditional thinking about middle aged female consumers and be prepared to add value to my shopping experience, he would have added value to his employer as well. After all, the cost to his employer in wages was the same, whether the salesman added value – or not – to the customer experience. I've said it before and will say it again: Get every employee involved in solutions to make sure you and they add value – not cost!

25

Don't just upsell – right sell

All kinds of businesses add value to their traditional services.

It's passion that leads suppliers to profit and add true value through suggested 'add-ons' and 'upselling' to a customer. I often have pretty definite views about what I want and I don't appreciate some high-powered salesperson trying to dissuade me to a different point of view. However, I certainly do value it when I sense they are listening carefully and fully comprehend my requirements, while gently offering suggestions on enhancements. Two examples come readily to mind.

One was an instance when I wished to produce some audio cassettes many years ago. A couple of producers gave quotes as per my specifications but one did far more. He took the time to ask questions and showed a genuine interest in my project. He offered suggestions and diplomatically challenged some false assumptions I had made. As a result, we established an excellent working partnership and the final product was much better than if it had been done exactly to my specifications. He truly added value by bringing his expertise to bear. My costs were greater than initially planned but because his suggestions added more value to my customers, I saw it more as an investment than an extra cost. Also, because of the time the supplier invested in me, he was re-engaged to convert the tapes to CDs many years later.

A printer did something similar with a poster I wanted produced. Rather than simply take the job order to run off the required copies, he suggested lamination, which I had not even considered. Yes, it cost more but the end result offered better value to my clients – a classic win/win scenario, because some customers don't always know the relatively low cost of services that you can offer to give them an even better solution to their initial needs.

Both instances admittedly added marginally more cost to me – but significant more value. That's not just up-selling – it's right-selling.

26

Measure twice-cut once

My mother was marvellous seamstress – a talent that bypassed me by a country mile. She was a product of the Great Depression where it probably wasn't feasible for her family to buy clothes off the rack. She darned socks, and refashioned my father's trousers (when he had literally worn out the seat of his pants) into boy's pants for church bazaars. In many ways, Mum was recycling out of necessity – or habit – long before the word was in the lexicon.

She made most of my dresses and patiently showed me how to cut a pattern, hand-baste the stitches and then sew the garment together on the machine – alas, I lacked any such precision and patience and would often ruin the material in my haste to get a finished product.

She'd scold: 'Measure twice. Cut once.' It was an old tailor's maxim, no doubt, which fell on deaf ears at the time, but it's amazing how many times I've heard those words echo in my ears since, even though I've never been near a sewing machine in decades.

However, the same principle applies to cutting paper – not corners – in the office. Or taking a moment to check that the letterhead is loaded the right way up in the printer before printing multiple copies. Or checking that a book or document fits into the envelope or box *before* you put the address on the package.

It's the same for tradesmen cutting a piece of timber or tile without first double checking the dimensions, or buying a fridge or washing machine only to discover it doesn't fit into the wall cavity. I always have a measuring tape in my home, office and car – and usually my handbag.

Having moved office and home, it's amazing how much back strain (not to mention stress!) that I've been able to save the removalists and myself by first measuring where the desk may best fit with the filing cabinets or bookshelves – even though I'm reasonably spatial, an approximate guess can result in a lot of un necessary effort if you're only a centimetre out of whack. You're probably paying the removalists by the hour so a little measurement early on can result in big costs savings later. By the way, when measuring furniture, be sure and take into account the base boards and measure from the narrowest point and both ends of the wall space – not just the middle.

27

The cost of re-work

'A job worth doing is worth doing well.' If I had a dollar for every time I heard my father say that when I was a girl, I'd be a wealthier woman today. In those days, when he employed me as a dishwasher and insisted that no piece of cutlery had a single streak, I simply thought: 'What would he know?

As it turns out, he knew a lot more than I thought he did.

One day, he discovered a tiny little lipstick mark on a glass and rather than simply have me re-wash that one, insisted I re-wash – and dry – the entire tray of glasses on my own time! It was a lesson I didn't appreciate – nor ever forgot.

He explained that it wasn't simply the cost of re-washing a little lipstick mark but that if a diner returned an expensive glass of wine – because of that little lipstick mark, that wine was wasted forever; and possibly longer term profits down the drain if the customer didn't return or told others that the dishes weren't clean.

Think of the cost of re-work in your organisation. There must be hundreds of examples:

- someone who simply hits the print button on the photocopier for 100 copies, without first checking that the original is correctly aligned so that it isn't produced upside down

- the painter who slaps on a coat of paint before taking a bit of time to prepare the surface properly; and then needs to go back and strip the paint, sand and re-apply
- the hairdresser who mixes the wrong colours and a brunette becomes a red head (yes, this happened to me)
- the mechanic who forgets to replace the oil cap
- the telemarketer or shipping clerk who carelessly mixes up customer order numbers and ships the wrong goods
- a tiny error of misplacing a component on a production line – and then everything needs to be reassembled
- addressing an express-paid envelope only to discover that the documents are too large to fit in it
- the report writer who doesn't proofread (or have someone else do so) and prints thousands of documents with an incorrect decimal place (there's a big difference between $10,000 and $100,000!)

OK, I know some readers might just find a little typo in this book. For example, spell check doesn't make allowances for 'from' slipping through as 'form', but if so, it won't alter the entire meaning of the manuscript – and there's no need to instantly re-print.

However, if a printer makes a tiny mistake on one little digit of a phone number, the entire batch of letterhead is useless. This happened with a printer I once used – and only used once! He offered me a 50% discount which of course I rejected – the correct phone number was essential on my company letterhead – so he had to reprint the whole batch at his expense, eroding his profit.

He had also made a mistake with the colour of my logo on the envelopes but I accepted those at a reduced price because I didn't figure a green or black logo on an envelope (which is often not opened by the recipient, anyway) was vital to my brand.

However, I never used that printer again. Most customers (including me) usually give someone a second chance if they make good their error, but he did so begrudgingly. I had used that same printing franchise for years, under previous ownership, and all my records should have still been accurately stored on their files, so it should have been simple to continue, but if he couldn't get it right with all my files that were already on record, I certainly didn't trust him with anything new.

Many years ago, another printer somehow managed to insert about 1/8 of pages in a book in the wrong order in about 25% of the 3,000 copies printed. He pointed out that this never 'should' have happened with their automated print processes – but somehow it did. I'd checked a few books in the first box opened and assumed everything was fine; we only discovered the error when a reader pointed it out months later. It was also assumed that it may have just been a problem with one box but worse still, it was an intermittent problem and the printer had to go through about 100 boxes of books, by hand, to weed out the problem books. To his credit, he did so and credited me with the dud books; but what a (hidden) cost of labour to his company to rectify. We still do business together and I would highly recommend him.

The old Australian attitude of: 'She'll be right mate' needs to shift to 'Get it right mate.' Get it right – first time, every time – by your customers.

Or, as my dear old Dad would add: 'Near enough is not good enough – only good enough is good enough.' OK, Dad ... now, I know you're right.

Do the right thing. And do things right.

28

Be responsible – and response-able

Empowerment encourages employees to be more responsible for the outcomes in the organisation. The ultimate objective is to have them feel that every action they take is what they would do if they owned the business. To do this, they must first understand that they 'own' the problem.

As I mentioned over 15 years ago, when 'Good Service is Good Business' became a #1 bestseller, if employees are to feel truly responsible, the organisation must also make everyone feel response-able. There should be the fewest possible barriers to prevent staff from acting in a responsible manner.

Does your organisation have unnecessary procedures and bureaucratic rules?

Be honest. Certainly it is necessary to follow certain compliance procedures which vary with the nature and size of the operation, but how many of those in place are actually required? Were some introduced many years ago only to remain long after their usefulness has been served?

Make it safe for employees to raise questions and offer suggestions. Leaders ask the tough questions and don't shy from the tough answers or shoot the proverbial messenger.

Many years ago, when Jan Carlzon was CEO of Scandinavian Airlines, he turned the airline around from an operating loss to an operating profit within 18 months. In his legendary book, 'Moments of Truth', he asked all employees to focus on minor improvements in their own area of the operation. He made front line staff responsible and response-able. For example, it used to take no fewer than nine signatures on a form to enable a flight attendant to provide extra coffee and biscuits if the plane was delayed. Yet who was in the best position to determine whether or not it was appropriate to serve customers extra amenities during the delay? The flight attendant! Were those extra signatures adding value or cost?

Carlzon eliminated the multiple signatures on the form and only required the sign off from the flight attendant. This reduced the workload of eight people, reduced the printing cost and significantly reduced the frustration of the person at the front line who had to put up with unnecessary red tape.

Carlzon went further to say that it was also acceptable if attendants wished to offer champagne and caviar to business class passengers. Most middle management thought this was a recipe for disaster and didn't credit flight attendants with the necessary judgment. Certainly, if attendants had provided champagne when a flight was delayed a few minutes, the airline would have been in financial difficulty. But they acted responsibly and only broke open the bubbly if it was warranted to appease passengers.

Is it possible that middle management saw the elimination of the nine signatures as a threat to their own jobs and sense of importance? The fact of the matter is that most employees would rather give good service than poor service.

29

The domino effect – don't check your brains in when you come to work

Unfortunately, not every employee shares that sense of common sense excellence. I'd returned home exhausted one rainy Friday evening – both the plane and the luggage arrived extremely late. Although frustrated, I wasn't at all upset with the airline as I understood the adverse weather conditions, that Friday night was their peak travel time and that they were doing their best in difficult circumstances.

The next day I had another flight with the same airline on a bright sunshiny Saturday morning. The plane sat on the runway for 20 minutes, for no apparent reason. I politely inquired as to what was causing the delay. 'Oh, catering has stuffed up again,' the flight attendant snapped. 'There's a Muslim family on board and catering forgot their special meal.'

I'm sure she said it to deflect any blame from her, without realising that by knocking other members of her airline team, she made herself look bad as well.

After another 20 minutes passed, we were still sitting there and the flight attendant was obviously also distressed, so I suggested that since it was only a one hour flight she could offer the family a free meal voucher in a restaurant at the other end, an upgrade on their next flight or some other form of compensation? I even joked that they could have the vegetarian meal I'd ordered for that day, because in terms of priorities, it seemed silly to hold up a plane of 200 people because a special meal was missing for four passengers, although it may have been a problem for a longer flight. She looked at me as if I had two heads and responded: 'I've already offered them free drinks, according to our guidelines'.

As I patiently pointed out that Muslims don't drink alcohol and she should consider another solution, she told me in no uncertain terms that she was 'in charge' of the in-flight service. Ha! She wouldn't have a clue about the meaning of the word. The plane was now three quarters of an hour late for a one hour flight and everyone's patience had worn thin.

When I arrived to speak at a conference, I asked how many other people had experienced delayed flights on that airline and most in the room put up their hands. I then explained that this was simply because one flight attendant had checked her brains in when she arrived at work that day and wouldn't use common sense. not only was my flight delayed, but so too was the return flight and then the next flight going back to the conference destination and so on. The domino effect of that dumb decision impacted upon not just the customers - but her co-workers all day long.

I later found out, by talking to staff members on the return flight, that there were, in fact, other options available to them in such situations but apparently this particular flight attendant chose not to use them.

Even if she had been correctly intentioned (which I don't believe she was) in terms of trying to save the airline a few dollars by not offering a few meal vouchers to four passengers, she cost the airline dearly in terms of 200 disgruntled customers on that flight and ultimately extra overtime staffing costs when all planes that day ended up behind schedule, inconveniencing thousands of passengers.

She was not part of the solution – but a major part of the problem.

30

Bust bureacracy

If employees feel they have some responsibility and are in a position to be able to help the customer, they are more likely to act in a responsible manner. It's very demeaning and de-motivating if front-line personnel are burdened with a strict policy which they must implement, regardless of the situation.

Many times, front-line people know what should be done to create a win/win situation to add major value to the customer with only minor cost to the company. However the rule book states that anything outside the norm must be referred to a supervisor, who has all too often insulated themselves from the customers and the frontline staff. When the customer then explains the same problem to the supervisor, often the response is: 'Oh yes, we can fix that'.

The intonation in the voice often implies that the front line employee should have done so in the first place. This not only damages staff morale but creates additional and unnecessary frustration and time delays for the customer.

I've heard it estimated that 70% of customers are satisfied if they only need to deal with one employee to fix their complaint. If a second person is involved, the satisfaction rate drops to 61% and diminishes further if their complaint continues to be passed to someone else. By eliminating unnecessary bureaucracy, you can create a better environment for both employees and customers.

Nominate someone from your team to become a red-tape renegade. Give them six months to cut out as much bureaucracy and complexity as possible from both your internal communications and the interactions you have with your customers and suppliers.

31

Break the management mould – make everyone responsible for quality value

A Melbourne-based company, Victa, specialises in the production of plastic injection moulds. Quality control is a vital part of their operation to ensure strict safety controls. Some years ago, three people were employed solely to inspect the finished products, ensure faulty goods were not delivered to the customer and to find the source of any problem. In spite of these rigid controls, major quality assurance problems continued.

In a change of strategy, management redeployed the three inspectors into the mainstream of the workforce. They announced to employees that the three inspectors were being 'sacked' and over 30 'inspectors' being hired in their place. The 30 inspectors were, in fact, the existing workforce. Everyone was made to feel responsible for inspecting their own part of the work in progress. The 'police' were eliminated. As a result, not only was there a decrease in reject products and an increase in overall quality, but absenteeism was significantly reduced.

Most employees like to feel part of the solution - not part of the problem.

32

If you're not part of the solution – you're part of the problem

Contrast this example to that of an unnamed public servant who sat next to me on a flight. He informed me that he paid $450 for a return flight, compared with the $180 I paid. Rules within his department stated he must book seven days in advance through the internal travel department on a full economy fare.

'It's not only a waste of taxpayers' money, but I can't respond quickly to customer requests, and then they think it's me who is hopeless,' he told me in frustration.

When asked why he didn't inform senior management, instead of me, about the obvious benefit of changing the rules, especially in view of increased airline competition, he responded: 'It's no use telling the powers that be. They don't care what happens in the field. They're only interested in creating rules to ensure they have something to do.'

I quickly lost my original sympathy to his plight. If you complain about your company and don't bother to offer suggestions for improvement, you have no right to complain. If you're not part of the solution, you are only adding cost – not value – to your organisation.

Bear in mind that management can't possibly implement every suggestion, so please don't be discouraged.

33

One person's trash is another person's treasure

I presume that this saying initially arose long before people frequented garage sales, scoured the streets before a council clean up or bought used goods at auctions or on e-bay; all excellent enough ways to save money if you enjoy doing it and/or have the time to do so.

I tend to place more value on my time than the actual dollars I might save. However, if I was more cash-poor and less time-poor, I'd likely utilise these outlets more.

I've learned over the years that we all tend to place a different value on our time and our possessions, according to our own rationale – which isn't always rational!

A friend thinks I'm extravagant to spend money on a lovely pen to use at book signings, pointing out that a $200 pen doesn't write any better than a five dollar one. He's absolutely right – yet he'll spend twice as much to buy a signed rugby jersey for his office wall!

34

One person's time is one person's time-opportunity cost

I know a wealthy man who drives over 30 kilometres to save three cents a litre on petrol. I'm unlikely to drive more than a block out of my way but I do try to purchase earlier in the week when it is generally a lower price (and if there isn't a big queue at the bowsers). *If* conveniently located, I tend to go to outlets that give me a discount with my shopping docket. He, on the other hand, says that's a female thing as he doesn't have a handbag to hold such dockets. I point out that I actually conveniently keep mine in the glove box of the car (although admittedly, some expiry dates have long since passed).

Ironically, he has a car which is substantially more expensive than mine (in fact, he has two cars when he really only needs one – but that's another story) Yet he thinks *I'm* extravagant by flying business class for more than a three hour flight. He's possibly right but because I have a lower back injury, it is worth every cent to me to have a flat bed and to arrive at my destination without pain.

On the other hand it would be a real pain for me to drive 30 kilometres to save three cents a litre on petrol. We both believe the other has flawed logic – but by the same token, we're both right according to our own values of what adds cost or value to our lives.

In *The Economic Naturalist: Why Economics Explains Almost Everything,* Robert H Frank (2008 Virgin Books, London) explains: 'If you ever took an economics course, you at least heard the term 'opportunity cost'. The opportunity cost of engaging in an activity is the value of everything you must give up to pursue it.'

Frank gives the following example: You are about to buy a $10 alarm clock at the shop on campus next door when a friend tells you that the same clock is available for five dollars at the supermarket in town. Do you go to town and get the clock for five dollars? Or do you buy it at the shop on campus? In either case, if the clock malfunctions under warranty, you must send it to the manufacturer for repairs.

'Of course,' he concludes, 'there is no universally right or wrong answer. each person has to weigh the relevant costs and benefits.'

Tick-tock, tick-tock ... We're all living on borrowed time. It's simply a question of *when* we will die – a question most of us will never know the answer to. The average life expectancy for an Australian male is 78.7 years and a female 83.5 years. So, even if you're a healthy 40 year old male, *statistically* you only have

43 more birthdays to celebrate, 2,236 more weekend golf games and 11,395 more sleeps til it's game over – statistically speaking. With this finite existence, there's clearly little time to waste.

So it's worth thinking about how we invest our money and time. We'll re-visit this a bit later, but ask yourself: are you spending yours as wisely as you might?

35

Paper clips don't grow on trees

Our notions of cost and value change over the years, as do our value systems and circumstances.

About 20 years ago I was a member of Sydney Rotary Club and met many delightful people through that association. One such gentleman was Paul Cotton, the then New Zealand Consul General.

He was dignified, urbane and successful – at the top of his profession; which is probably why over two decades later, I vividly recall a story that seemed somewhat out of character with his distinguished diplomatic posting.

One day at lunch, he proudly proclaimed that he had never spent a cent on the purchase of paper clips.

'I figure that as many paper clips must come into the office as go out of the office so I insist that staff remove them, prior to throwing the paper in the bin.'

Remember, this was long before the days of recycling being popular. At the time, I must confess that I thought this was a rather odd, penny pinching practice. After all, I was an IBM executive, during a stage of rapid growth, and felt that the cost of paper clips was pretty inconsequential to a larger organisation.

How wrong I was!

Many years later, I still think of that story and now view both the principle and the person in a totally different light. Paul was certainly not an eccentric and thrifty bureaucrat but a visionary – both economically and ecologically.

Even such a small saving was hugely signaficant because it actually signalled a much bigger shift in the mindset of every employee.

Just like Mum often chastised me that money didn't grow on trees, likewise ... paper clips don't grow on trees!

This made me curious about the origins of the paper clip.

A Google search proved fascinating but confusing, as there was little agreement on Wikipedia and other sites as to who invented the paperclip. It seems there were several patents filed in the late 1800s and early 1900s in Norway, the UK and the USA. I'll leave the ownership debate to others but the paperclip has certainly been around for a long time.

Its prime purpose was to replace paper and string when bundling piles of paper. Today, these ubiquitous office supplies are so versatile that there are even claims on the internet that only one in ten paper clips are used for their intended purpose. They are commonly called on to clean out crevices, re-set electronic devices, hold up hems and twiddle into various shapes as a form of stress relief!

It became far more than a fastener in Norway during World War II. Prohibited from wearing anything with the king's initials, Norwegians wore paper clips on their lapels to show national unity and opposition to the German occupation.

Let's show international solidarity to put paper clip thinking into practice and cut unnecessary costs. Let's adopt paperclip productivity and pursue paperclip profitability. Like the humble paperclip, this concept can, literally, help hold our organisations together. Of course, this means I'll never be invited to address the Paper Clip Manufacturers conference – but c'est la vie!

36

Another old fashioned recycling tip

Paper doesn't grow on trees either (figuratively speaking), so if the paper that comes into your office is clean, reusable and not confidential, why not quickly place it in a tray conveniently located near where you open the mail? When you have a pile, you can easily cut pages of standard A4 sheets in half or quarters and staple together for a notepad. Saves money, saves trees and costs very little time – probably no more time than going to the store to buy a new notepad.

37

Handle paper only once

The previous example may slightly break the old adage of handling paper only once. Again I emphasise that it is vital to consider the value of your time – the most valuable asset any of us have in life.

There are entire books written on time management (a bit more on that later), but they all agree that we should handle paper only once – act on it, delegate it, file it or bin it. The same principle applies to emails.

38

Re-phrase to re-think

When confronted with any cost cuts, we tend to think in a negative sense so maybe it's timely to take a more positive approach and re-think how we encourage employees and others along a more cost conscious path.

I don't know about you but I'm one of those people who gets annoyed – if not downright defensive – when other people tell me what I 'should' do. Most of us are much more receptive to suggestions along the lines that we 'might consider an alternative approach' or 'look at things a little differently'.

It doesn't need to be a case of abundance or scarcity.

Let's shift the tone from one of saying, 'Don't buy anything' (paperclips or whatever) to, 'Isn't it amazing that we haven't needed to buy paperclips for X months.'

Rather than say: 'All employees must turn out the lights,' ask: ' Let's see if we can save enough on energy costs next month to have a staff night out at the movies?'

Talk to your employees to let them understand the true financial position as they may be more willing to make cuts if they understand the facts and this will also help reduce workplace rumours.

39

Real estate – real value or real costly?

When I first left IBM to start a micro business, I felt the need for a prestigious office space located in the central business district if my largely corporate clients were to take me seriously – or if not an actual office, certainly an address in the CBD. I quickly discovered that it made no difference whatsoever to my sort of business, as many clients who I spoke for at conferences were interstate or overseas anyway. It was neither necessary nor practical for them to meet in person. Credibility didn't require a corner office.

In fact, I later learned there was no need for me to even visit Sydney clients in their office; instead I found it more productive to take a more comprehensive client briefing over the phone, with access to all resources in my office. This meant reduced travel time for me, and neither the client nor I 'wasted' time in idle chit-chat over a cup of coffee (although, naturally it's beneficial to also have face to face relationships).

Your work location depends on the nature of your business – and the nature of your personality.

Do you need an expensive office in the central business district; a workplace closer to your home or customers; or a home office/workplace?

Obviously, if it's important for high traffic and high visibility, the higher cost of occupying a shopfront on a major street is good value. However, if your business is mainly referrals and not subject to casual passing trade, there would be no obvious reason to occupy prime real estate. In fact, passers-by could be a distraction from your main game. I learned this when I relocated from the CBD to a street front near my home at Manly Beach – where my otherwise wonderful PA at the time was often distracted by gorgeous guys changing into their wetsuits outside our window (OK, I was too).

After a brief stint of working from home, I discovered it wasn't right for me, at that point in time, for a number of reasons, including too many distractions in the form of the fridge, the garden etc.

An off-street, quiet office space overlooking nothing but tree tops proved so perfect for me that I actually bought it, rather than pay rent.

However, working from home is perfect for others. One needs to weigh up the cost of time travelled versus the cost of time wasted if constantly interrupted by children; neighbours; or your own lack of discipline. Just ask the question. There are no right or wrong answers. The question is only what is best for you? Just think through what's right for you before signing a long lease.

This principle applies not just to small business but also to big businesses looking to reduce their real estate expenditure. It started many years ago in Japan where rents were hundreds of thousands of yen per square metre in space-poor Tokyo. Sales staff traditionally each had their own desk, despite being primarily on the road. These were replaced with portable file cabinets that were wheeled into a rotating/allocated work station when the employee was actually in the office, according to a roster.

These days, technology has *theoretically* enabled greater work/life balance of the work force and has resulted in many large- and medium-sized organisations offering employees the option to work from home on a part time or almost full time basis. This has not only helped retain some workers (mainly those responsible for child care or elder care) but has also often reduced the real estate costs to employers. Again, it is always necessary to weigh up the savings against any potential disruption of working from a virtual location. It is also important for employees to take personal responsibility for managing that work/life balance, rather than feeling obliged to be connected to technology 24/7 – but that's another story.

If you have one or two major clients, another option may be to lease space – or do a contra deal – on their premises. A computer technician was so valued by a client that they leased a permanent monthly parking space for him at their CBD premises as they actually found it was cheaper than paying an hourly parking fee for him.

Do you need a high rent CBD office; a less expensive and probably larger work place in the suburbs near home or major customers; or can you work efficiently from your home or garage – at virtually no dollars and cents cost?

40

No real estate but real value – mobility of suppliers

Most people in business – large or small – are time-poor. Most starting out in a small business are also cash-poor – very cash-poor. They may be hesitant to commit to a long lease or not be able to afford a deposit for premises. However, rather than see this as a problem in serving their customer set, it could be an actual advantage in some instances, if marketed properly.

For example, for many years, I was loyal to a great hairdresser in the neighbourhood where I used to live. Even when I relocated 15 kilometres away, I still travelled to her salon as I didn't want to risk a 'bad hair' day when I was speaking at a conference or doing media interviews for a book. I felt it was important to look the same as the photos on my website. Even though I resented the time in traffic, I was still willing to not only travel-but to pay top dollar for her services.

I was a loyal customer and she never gave me a reason to change. However, on one occasion, I was in desperate need of a cut and she was overseas so I used another hairdresser at the same salon – but not with the same outcome, even though I had paid the same high price.

Coincidentally, I caught up with a friend that evening and complimented her on her hair, which was a similar style to mine and looked sensational.

'Where did you get it done?'

I was stunned when she smugly replied: 'At home.'

I discovered that she used a mobile hairdresser so I rather warily decided to give this unknown person a try, since my own cut wasn't up to scratch and it would be weeks before my normal hairdresser returned.

Much to my surprise, I was delighted with the result and (no surprise at all) overjoyed with the cost. not only was it approximately half the cost of a cut and colour in the city salon, but I had no travel time and no parking fees. Admittedly, I didn't get a 'free' cappuccino – but with the savings, I could buy espressos for every day of the month!

What's more, I had my choice of background music, didn't have to hear other blow driers whirring noisily, and rather than read gossip magazines while my foils was setting, I used those 20 minutes to do something productive and prepare dinner.

Of course, I probably could have called a mobile chef to do it for me! Or a mobile mechanic to service my car. Or a mobile masseuse to work out the tension in my neck muscles from too much time writing at a computer.

All of those services would be substantially less costly than if I went to their premises as they have no rental overheads and I have no travel time and no waiting time – win/win as they say. Same skills, lower overheads, better margin for them, and better value for me.

I recommended the mobile hairdresser to a number of friends but interestingly only a few use her because, as one married friend with young children emphatically states: 'Oh no, I love going to the salon because that's time out for me. I actually always tell my husband that it takes an hour longer than it actually does!'

To me, extra time is better than champagne, caviar and chocolate combined – the one luxury I crave most but never seem to have enough of. As well as savings to buy the champers, the mobile hairdresser gave me the gift of time – yet it wasn't perceived as such by my married friend. This again goes to prove that we simply need to continually ask the question of our business, our customers and our suppliers: Value or cost? Value or cost? Value or cost?

41

Wombat – don't waste your advertising $

I believe it was Lord Leverhulme who first pronounced that half of his money spent on advertising was wasted – he just didn't know which half! I put to you that all of your advertising budget could potentially be wasted if you don't deliver the actual product or service in line with the promised expectation of the experience.

In an earlier book, *The Customer Service Zoo,* I introduced the terminology of WOMBAT marketing, though the actual principle is age old. WOMBAT stands for **W**ord **O**f **M**outh – **B**est **A**dvertising **T**echnique.

Research shows that it costs five times more to acquire a new customer than it does to retain an existing one. Yet, how often do organisations launch expensive mass marketing campaigns to attract new customers while failing to allocate the necessary resources to look after the ones that they already have?

Banks and telecommunications companies have traditionally been notorious for this and only get away with it because of the huge volume of customers they churn in near monopoly situations. Few other businesses could survive with that approach.

My bank recently advertised an attractive interest rate on a savings account in the national media. It was almost a percentage point more than what I was receiving but when I called to enquire I was informed that it was only a 'honeymoon rate' for new customers.

'Hmmm, this seems like a marriage where I'm being taken for granted – I may have to divorce myself from your bank,' I joked. Frankly, I had no intention of doing so as I detest filling in forms and am one of the few people I know who is generally pretty pleased with my bank. Much to my surprise, my banking relationship manager replied: 'Well, because you've been such a good customer, I'd be happy to extend that rate to you.' One wonders if they lost any customers who didn't bother to call but simply transferred their money to another banking facility for the honeymoon period. Surely there must be extra costs to the bank of setting up new accounts and closing old ones.

Don't get me wrong – I truly believe that a great advertising campaign can certainly build brand awareness and market longevity, as evidenced by such world-renowned brands as Coca Cola, Nike and American express.

However, it's vital for the vitality of your brand that the service delivery actually lives up to the *promise* of your advertising. If you plan to be in business for the long haul, it is no strategy to over-promise and under-deliver. You may spend a lot of money on TV commercials, glossy colour magazines or the coolest of cool websites – but if one person tells another that they tried your product and it didn't live up to expectations, is that potential new customer more likely to believe their friend/colleague or your fancy campaign? If you don't deliver on your promise, did your campaign add value or cost to your bottom line?

The answer is obvious. Advertising dollars don't add up – if your product and brand don't measure up.

However, you can't hide your light under a bushel either – so combine great advertising with great products and great service. But make sure you get the last two firmly functional before spending much on the first.

The huge growth in viral marketing through social media and networking further supports the power of word of mouth advertising. It's not the topic of this book but we'll mention it briefly later on.

42

Direct mail or direct to bin

Frank Prestipino, former Vice President of Oracle, writes in *Getting to Big the Small Way* (McGraw Hill, 2008): 'Often our perception of the value we offer in a business transaction, and the things that our customers actually value, can be widely different. It is actually far worse to send generic marketing material that adds no value, such as a piece of direct mail, than to not send anything at all.'

This can be the case if overdone but I, for one, don't mind receiving so-called 'junk mail' in my letter box at home as I'm an infrequent shopper and can easily flick though marketing fliers to see what's on offer while watching the news.

I was recently bemused to receive an expensive glossy folder advertising an ecologically friendly product. Their marketing material and core message were so obviously not aligned.

While we're on the topic of direct mail, make sure that mailing lists and data bases are kept as up to date as possible (easier said than done when you don't always know that someone has moved). not only do you waste postage for snail mail but even if you use electronic mailing lists, it makes you appear unprofessional and annoys stakeholders to receive incorrectly addressed mail.

One acquaintance claims to have received no less than seven pieces of mail from different parts of the same organisation within one week.

Of course, spam is illegal so don't even go there!

Advertising is powerful. Marketing makes sales. Just make sure your message matters to your target audience.

43

The true value of trust

Professor Fred Hollows was a well respected eye surgeon in Sydney who volunteered to give thousands of underprivileged people in the Australian outback and developing countries the gift of sight through a relatively simple cataract procedure.

Now buried literally at the Back O' Bourke, he inspired many other medical practitioners to donate their time and expertise to those who could normally never afford their services.

One such friend of a friend is a highly respected dentist who, for many years, has used his vacation to train dental surgeons in Cambodia. As a result, that country, still recovering from the atrocities of the horrific Pol Pot regime, is starting to build a reputation as a place to receive low cost but high quality dental work. As I planned to cycle around the ancient ruins of Angkor Wat, I contemplated also having a crown on one of my teeth at a fraction of the cost of such elective surgery in Australia.

Prior to booking my trip, I happened to be reading an excellent book, titled *Flip,* by fellow speaker Peter Sheahan. In one chapter, he wrote about the relationship between trust and cost and cited his own experience with laser eye surgery.

Two of his friends had it done. One paid $6,000 in Sydney, whereas his other friend had surgery in Kuala Lumpur at 1/5 the price. Both operations were successful, resulting in 20/20 vision.

Peter did more research and discovered that both places used the same equipment and both surgeons trained in Australia. He was headed to Kuala Lumpur so even had his flight costs covered. It seemed a simple choice. Did he pay $1,200 or $6,000?

He writes that he paid $6,000 and would do so again in a heartbeat because after questioning the Sydney surgeon he knew that if anything happened to go wrong, the Sydney doctor would suffer more as he would be exposed to more negative media coverage.

Peter posed the question to the reader: 'Who would you trust with your sight – someone who lives and works in the same community or someone who lives thousands of miles away?'

It's an interesting twist on the notion of value or cost, as both operations proved good value – one at a fraction of the cost of the other. However, there was a perceived (and possibly real) additional risk to the overseas operation and most of us make important decisions, especially relating to health, not just on cost but on trust for both the immediate result and the long-term guarantee.

I know of a woman who had plastic surgery in Thailand and looks a million dollars at a fraction of the price. After all, I've had great haircuts, manicures and physiotherapy in countries where I haven't spoken a word of the language – and yet had a local manicurist ruin three finger nails. So why not get a crown for my tooth overseas?

No, I didn't have any dental work done in Cambodia, but if I hear of at least five other trusted friends who do so, I just might. It may bring a whole new meaning to the concept of word of mouth.

Did Peter and I make our decisions based on trust or fear? Who knows, but for me, there are some things you just can't quantify in terms of cost/value.

44

Re-engineer to build a better mouse trap

Inventor Edwin Land once remarked that 'people who seem to have had a new idea have often simply stopped having an old idea.'

I'm not an engineer and admire the mechanical know how of talented individuals who actually build things and figure out how various processes all work together. I tend to take all the behind the scenes processes for granted and still marvel that we can simply flick a switch to get electricity from some far flung generator, turn a little ignition key to make our cars start or drive safely over a suspension bridge.

Countless individuals around the world are always looking for better ways to make things – and make them happen more efficiently. Certainly, there are hundreds of technical text books and case studies available and it is not the intent of this book to explore that area.

However, I recently read a short article in a business magazine[1] that was simple enough for any lay person to understand. It was about a leading

---

1 Harvard Business Review on Green Business Strategy – 2007

maker of materials for commercial interiors. In its new Chinese carpet factory, a liquid had to be circulated through a pump similar to those used in almost all industries, worldwide. A top European company had designed this 'standard' system to use pumps requiring a total of 95 horse power. However, the engineer responsible for the carpet factory realised that two simple design changes would cut that power requirement to only seven horse power – a 92% reduction! His redesigned system cost less to build, involved no new technology and worked better in all respects.

What two design changes achieved this 12-fold saving in pumping power? First, he chose fatter than usual pipes which created much less friction than thin pipes and therefore needed far less pumping energy. Then he made the pipes short and straight instead of long and crooked. He did this by laying out the pipes first and then positioning the various tanks and boilers and the other equipment that they connected – fewer bends and again less friction. He looked at the entire system and this 'whole system thinking' could help other managers find small changes that lead to big savings that are cheap, free or even better than free (because they make whole systems cheaper to build).

45

Invent, re-invent or de-invent

When we think of invention, we think of geniuses – Edison, Einstein, Marconi. Rather than burn the candle at both ends trying to perfect it, Edison spent his time inventing the light bulb as an alternative source of light.

When we think of re-invention or re-engineering, we think of leaders who may not have their name attributed to a product or process, but who still made a contribution by improving what was once the status quo.

Could similar benefits be found in 'de-invention'? It's not even a proper dictionary word but what I mean by this is rather than just look at the things that delight your customers (important as it is) ... look at the little things which annoy them.

Organisations seldom receive everyday complaints or compliments about their vision, mission statement or strategic plan – their big picture stuff. Yet little things can drive you and your customers crazy – and may drive them away.

Think of times you've been in a bedroom with a mosquito buzzing around in the dark. Are there little things that your customers find pesky? Get out the equivalent of insect spray in your organisation and get rid of those little things that bug people.

We so often focus only on giving customers more. More isn't always better. Bigger isn't always better. Only better is better. Sometimes finite resources are inadvertently channelled into giving customers more, when they could be better spent eliminating small sources of annoyance.

Executives need to constantly weigh up the cost benefit of changing their products – of inventing, re-inventing or de-inventing.

It cost Coca Cola dearly when they tried to re-invent the 'new Coke' – most of us wanted the consistent taste of the old – or real – Coke.

With brands like Cadbury, Panadol or Bandaid, we expect them to stay much the same. The tradition, stability and safety are what we value. But with electronics, we want innovation and change – the latest and greatest gadget supersedes tradition.

Is it time to invent, re-invent or de-invent?

46

The cost of complexity

As companies grow and evolve, so too the internal working environment tends to become more complex. This is only natural as internal processes must evolve to cope with more customers and probably more staff. More transactions and interactions usually result in more complexity. Growth is good but can be overwhelming for some individuals and may indeed generate an added, yet often hidden, cost of complexity.

What can be done? Systems are useful and generally enhance productivity. Just make sure that you don't make them overly complicated, which may ultimately result in more work and less efficiency.

Systemise and document as much as you can but involve your own staff members, who are the end users of the system, from the start. Don't simply delegate holus bolus to some external consultant who may, with every good intention, create a monster that is unmanageable on a day-to-day basis.

Outsiders can undoubtedly provide invaluable insight and input as they are able to take more of a holistic helicopter view of your organisation. They don't wear the 'blinkers' of long-serving employees, and are able to offer a different perspective from a broader, overall analysis. Just make sure that they involve all relevant staff (not just managers) in the process to ensure that plans on paper are indeed operationally practical.

The old KISS (Keep It Simple, Stupid) principle should always be your first option in order to avoid any unwarranted costs of complexity.

After all, I suspect that if the humble paperclip were invented today, it might have 27 moving parts, three microchips and need upgrades twice a year!

47

What gets measured gets done

The same applies to measurement. There is little doubt that what gets measured gets done; that employees focus on management measurements of performance; and that owners, boards and political masters rightly request measurement of overall organisational performance from their management team.

Quantifiable accountability is vital. Targets and benchmarks are important. But it's equally critical to consider the cost of complexity; to ensure that you don't waste precious time in overly-complicated measurement.

Weigh up the cost and benefit of any proposed measurement system. Speaking of weight, for example ... We may have a reasonable target to lose three kilograms of body weight in a month and scales can obviously measure that progress. However, it's of no benefit to the final outcome if we get on the scale five times a day! Nor is it helpful if we buy a fancy $300 scale when a $30 one is probably as accurate as we need (since we're not measuring, say, a fraction of an ounce of gold).

The scales will indeed help us measure our progress but this simply needs to be done, at the most, once a day, at the same time with the same clothing – comparing apples with apples.

The same principle applies to any organisational gauges. Keep them as simple as possible to make sure any measurements are meaningful and add value – not cost – to the desired outcome.

I know of an organisation that devised such a complicated commission structure for sales representatives that one of their top performers freely admitted that he spent almost as much time trying to figure out how to 'play the game' to maximise his bonuses and special incentives for trips and awards, as he did in face to face interaction to sell high end products to the actual customer.

Certainly, employee rewards for tangible and measured results are excellent incentives. Just make sure that they don't detract from them – or you – keeping their eye on the ball: the bottom line customer results. KISS, KISS, KISS!

48

Is necessity the mother of invention?

A financial planner friend started his working life in the advertising business in the United Kingdom and shared the following story:

As he tells it, Boots, one of the largest chemist chains in the UK, commenced manufacture of their home brand of aspirin many years ago. Each bottle was precisely filled with say, 30 tablets and cotton wool was then inserted so that the pills didn't move and therefore crumble into powder.

After some time, they realised that it was actually cheaper to pack the bottle full of tablets than source the cotton wool from another supplier. This proved not only a win for them but a win for the customer – the customer got more pills and Boots got more profit.

In that instance, the cotton wool only added more cost – not value. Ironically, the change may have been instigated as a result of an existing supplier being unable to meet demand. Thus, an obstacle became an opportunity through a paradigm shift in thinking about how to best pack the pills. This is often the case, as per Plato's pronouncement that necessity is the mother of invention.

I asked why they didn't simply use smaller bottles in the first place? Apparently, there was already a ready supply of the 'standard' bottle so it would have been more costly to manufacture a smaller one.

49

Why drive through banks have braille keypads

Have you ever wondered why drive-through banks have Braille keypads installed? After all, the keypad is located on the driver's side of the car and the driver, if sight impaired, surely would not be driving a motor vehicle!

This conundrum was simply explained in *The Economic Naturalist: Why Economics Explains Almost Everything* (2008 Virgin Books, London):

British author, Robert H Frank, outlines that the patrons of these machines are almost always drivers, none of whom are blind. However, according to his former student, Bill Tjoa, cash point manufacturers are obliged to make keypads with Braille dots for their walk-up machines anyway so there was, indeed, no greater cost to also have them at drive throughs.

50

Give to get – re-framed thinking

We've been focused on reducing costs. On the flip side of the coin, what if you gave away a few cents with no expectation of return – and gained thousands of dollars worth of business within a few months?

Heading home from my morning cycle, I happened to pass an upmarket art gallery in Sydney. I felt under-dressed (i.e. sweaty lycra, looking more like My Favourite Martian, in an unflattering cycle helmet, than any patron of the arts). There were no other customers so I tentatively ventured in, thinking I might save myself a trip to the hardware store later in the day. Not only was I warmly greeted, but quite astonished when the owner refused to accept any payment for a metre of picture wire. That's probably why, a few months later, an organisation with which I was affiliated placed an order with that gallery for over $4,000 worth of framing. It's also why, many years later when I could finally afford it, I bought one of those expensive oil paintings I saw on that first day on my bicycle.

Nice guys don't finish last. Caring about customers pays. The picture wire only cost the owner a few cents, for which I would have gladly paid a few dollars as a standard transaction and never given it another thought. However, her unexpected generosity and attitude remained in my mind long after the event. Obviously, not everyone would return to buy a painting but the picture wire was minimal cost to her and the gesture highly perceived value by me.

51

Is it nuts to give away free peanuts or tea?

Have you ever wondered why some pubs charge customers over three dollars for a glass of water but give them free peanuts (especially when tap water is virtually free)?

Let me again paraphrase Robert H Frank, author of *The Economic Naturalist: Why Economics Explains Almost Everything:* (2008 Virgin Books, London)

Alcohol and peanuts are complements with each other. If you eat more salted nuts, you want more alcohol; and since nuts are relatively cheap and each alcoholic drink generates a relatively higher profit margin, publicans make peanuts free – meanwhile these freely available salty nuts tend to increase the profits of the bar.

By contrast, alcohol and water are competitors with each other. The more water customers drink, the fewer alcoholic beverages they will order. So even though water has virtually no cost associated with it, apart from supply and cleaning of glasses and a bit of labour, bars have an incentive to set a high price for it.

This reminds me about carpet and jewellery salesmen in many parts of the world, especially the

Middle East, who entice you into their store with the offer of a refreshing cup of tea or cool drink.

'No obligation, madam, please come in from the heat and be comfortable as my guest.' Of course, one does then indeed feel somewhat more obliged to buy an expensive rug or ring. You are seldom offered a complimentary drink in shops that sell low cost items as it would be a proportionately higher cost to the owner for the value he might eventually receive.

Water, tea or something else? Is there anything you can give away with little cost to you that is valued highly by your customers-and that may encourage them to spend more on your more profitable lines, or even just to spend more time on your premises?

52

Climate change or comfortable climate for business?

Myanmar (once known as Burma) is one of the poorest countries in the world, rife with political tension and still developing a modern day infrastructure where electricity outages are not uncommon. I have no idea how the managing director of a shipping company came across one of my earlier books but was delighted to receive an email from him out of the blue. His story is not directly related to cost but clearly shows the value proposition from the perspective of a developing country and the principle is worth developing in any nation. This is an extract from his email, bearing in mind that English isn't his first language (but that the language of great service is universal music to customer ears):

> 'My customers have faced enough troubles. Why would we make more? We make joke with them for the climate, road traffic, communications and daily matters. I figured that it can reduce their tension at certain time.
>
> 'For example, our office tower is out off electricity every day. Customers have to use stair to

arrive our office at 5th floor. You can imagine how they feel in hot weather. Therefore, I bought generator which can run air condition at reception room and also installed a water cooler and some ice wet towels. now, customers are pleased to come and stay for long time. We can make more talking with customers and able to know their requirements, difficulties and future prospects.

'Last Sunday, one customer called my wife. He ask to her to pick up his cargo and freight on Sunday because he will leave early Monday morning and not time to wait our office opening. My wife call me to pick up his cargo at hotel. I was in service station for checking my truck. Therefore, I went to hotel and met the customer without mentioning my designation because I only wore t-shirt and jeans.

'Customer passed the cargo and settled the freight to me. I gave him receipt with my signature. He thought that I was driver and contacted to my wife again that he had paid the money to delivery man. My wife replied to him not to worry because this driver is managing director of company and her husband! Customer was truly amazed and asked me to sit with him for coffee. He told me that he had contacted several other shipping lines that could not pick up Sunday and asked if it was regular for us. I said I was used to this service because most customers are tourists and contact us Saturday and Sunday, sometimes 10:00pm after dinner because they have shortage of time when they have to pack for leaving.

'To cut my letter short, this kind of thinking was born from your book, *[Good Service is Good Business]* I always share to my staffs as well and other colleagues indicating page 118, paragraph 5:

'ADD VALUE BY DOING THAT LITTLE BIT EXTRA

'Yours truly, Tommy Thant Sin – Managing Director Transocean Shipping Services Limited, Myanmar.'

Thank you, Tommy, for that example. You not only made your customer's day – you made mine by illustrating that many principles are universal and that wherever we live, it's possible to add a lot of value to your customers without adding a lot of cost to your bottom line.

53

Save cost and save the planet

There are many excellent publications that delve into great detail on saving costs and saving the environment through recycling materials, reducing energy consumption and implementing other eco-friendly measures. It is not the intent of this book to focus on these important actions and/or debate the relative speed of climate change. However, there is little question that the general sociological climate has indeed changed in terms of attitudes towards greater concern for the environment. Therefore, we've included some simple suggestions on saving costs that just happen to also contribute in some small measure toward saving the planet – the two need not be mutually exclusive.

It's important to recognise that it is easier for some organisations – and individuals – to be more 'green' in some areas than in others. For example, if your job is at a factory 50 miles away and no public transport is available, you have little choice but to take your car, whereas many of us are fortunate enough to have the option to use public transport, walk or cycle.

Although I've built an eco-friendly home and probably travel more miles on my bicycle annually than I do in my fuel-efficient car, I must confess to being a higher-than-average air traveller. I used to feel guilty when friends challenged me on carbon emissions from aircraft but then realised that just as some people take a bus to work, I must take a plane (public transport) to speak at conferences on the other side of the country or the world.

Although this personal disclosure may not be directly relevant to the thrust of this book, I felt it was apt to accept that it is virtually impossible to be 'environmentally perfect' in our Western world. I'm not suggesting that we all live in mud brick homes with no appliances; but that we can all contribute in many *small* ways by minor modifications to lifestyle.

54

Recycling – trendy or by necessity?

Almost every organisation – large or small – seems to be on the eco-friendly bandwagon. Yet many so-called 'leading edge' recycling trends are really nothing new. My grandparents grew their own vegetables, preserved pickles and jams in jars they had saved and wasted not a scrap of anything. During the Depression, I'm told that my grandmother recycled flour bags into dresses. A worn out dress could easily be reborn as an apron; that apron morphed into a dish towel before eventually used as a rag.

Hand-me-down clothes were the norm, along with darned socks and hand-knitted jumpers in days when the average housewife gave no thought to designer brands. Long before the days of compost bins, Grandma dug organic waste back into the garden.

My mother would carefully unwrap gifts to neatly fold and reuse the paper and ribbon. She did the same with kitchen foil, elastic bands and plastic bags.

In spite of attempts to make me feel guilty at the supermarket checkout, I still take home a percentage of groceries packed in plastic bags – shock, horror. However, these are then reused as garbage bin liners – rather than taking my groceries home in my recycled bag and then purchasing garbage bin liners from the supermarket shelf.

In the 'old days' handles were glued back on broken crockery. Lights were always switched off when not in use and leftovers from Sunday's roast formed the basis of Monday's Shepherd's pie.

Nothing was ever thrown out and waste was disparaged. To this day, I personally feel Mum overdid recycling somewhat when she gave me for breakfast what I refused to eat at dinner!

These generations of women before me were decidedly more cost conscious than environmentally conscious. Thankfully, the two don't need to be mutually exclusive. We just need to give a second thought to how we use our precious resources (whether household or global) – and if they are adding value at the time – as times change.

55

Paper or paperless?

Paper is one of the biggest forms of waste.

Use fewer paper napkins. Do you really need to grab a huge stack from the takeaway food outlet when you know you'll only use one or two? Surely the food outlet would reduce costs if they only handed out one napkin per purchase, rather than have freely available on top of the counter? Each American consumes an average of 2,200 standard two-ply napkins per year. If everyone in the US used an average of one fewer napkin per day, more than a billion pounds of napkins could be saved from landfills each year. A stack of napkins this size could fill the entire Empire State Building (*The Green Book: The Everyday Guide to Saving the Planet One Simple Step at a Time;* Elizabeth Rogers, Thomas M. Kostigen, 2007).

Much paper can now be recycled – this book is printed on recycled paper. However, that still means more energy was used to reprocess that recycled paper.

The technology has been available for some years which would enable you to read this on your computer or hand-held device. This may mean a higher initial cost to you to purchase the equipment but a lower cost for my publisher to produce and send this information electronically. This would ultimately lower the cost to the consumer to download the contents of the book. So does a hard copy book add value or cost?

Again, it all depends. And since 'it all depends' seems to be a recurring theme – and the IT world is full of acronyms – let's term this **IAD** (It All Depends) or maybe more simply, the **ID Premise.**

So do you need a hard copy book or an e-book? **ID** – **I**t **D**epends – on how savvy you are with technology, how long your battery life lasts, how advanced is the technology which might allow readers to highlight relevant text and write in the margins of a book when we think of an idea prompted by the author etc. I encourage you to write in the margins of books you buy (not library books), because an author's role is only to trigger your *own* thoughts to implement an idea.

I hate to say it, as authors only receive royalties when books are purchased new, but please feel free to go to your library or have a book swap with friends. I personally purchase and keep all non-fiction books as references because when I want to re-visit them, I can easily see the highlighted points at a glance and, occasionally, may even re-read an entire favourite book because I always discover something that didn't strike me as particularly relevant on the first reading.

However, I confess that about 50% of the novels I read aren't purchased new but swapped with friends or bought from a second hand shop as 'airplane' books that I leave on seats of terminals when finished. Although I'd enjoyed the novel at the time, it seldom has long-term value to take up space in my library.

On the other hand, some friends buy and keep every book. Others only borrow from the library – again a difference in value or cost proposition. I just ask you to think about your own.

56

Simply print – or im-print value

Does your printing add value or cost? Do you work with a good print company who understands your business and can advise on the best processes and options for your desired outcome? I do, and recently the printer suggested a means whereby I actually spent less to achieve the same result.

Can you use a different type or weight of paper that essentially looks the same? Is it possible and practical to print double sided copies?

Can you better market your services by printing on the back of a business card? Or do you wish to leave it blank so the recipient can write their own notes?

Can you recycle paper or use recycled paper?

Can you recycle print cartridges by having them re-filled? (I looked into this but the outlet was so far from my office it would have cost more in petrol and time than any potential savings to the bottom line or the environment.)

If you have a colour printer, does every document need to be printed in colour, or can you simply alter the settings to black and white preferences, as colour ink cartridges are more costly? Similarly, bold font uses more ink than normal font (although admittedly this is a miniscule amount).

Just think before you print – and consider whether you even need to print at all! Personally, I still find it more productive to print the final draft of a book and edit the manuscript with an old fashioned red pen in hand.

When was the last time you received a hand-written note or card in the post? Most of my client and personal communication is via email – which is both cheaper and faster, but every now and then I send a hand-written note (in spite of comments about my handwriting scrawl). I'm sure it's not appreciated by all clients but many have told me they've been thrilled to get something other than a bill in the post – so in this instance, rather than the cost of printing and postage, it may be viewed as a valued point of difference from the 'normal' email communication.

If you still use a fax machine, avoid a cover page where possible and you'll save paper at both ends of the transmission.

Some years ago, I was bemused when an airline handed out a full colour glossy menu on expensive cardboard, just before our flight took off. This was at the same time as media reports that airline faced financial woes. Since I liked the service on that carrier and hoped they'd remain in business, I thought I'd offer some free consulting.

I explained to the flight attendant that it seemed pointless to spend money on this menu when, in fact, the passenger had no choice!

'It's got nothing to do with me' she replied politely. (never an acceptable response!)

'You'll have to contact marketing with that complaint.'

I assured her that it wasn't a complaint – just one small idea to help the airline save a bit of money and possibly save her job. Sadly, they went bankrupt a few months later – certainly not because of the menus but due to other circumstances – and at least partially due to the fact that the front line, marketing, production and finance teams didn't communicate with each other.

Of course that would never happen in your organisation, would it?

Paul Simons, former Chairman of Woolworth, quoted Bill Wylie when he said:

'Businesses don't fail-people fail.'

Whether it's printing or not, always have it imprinted on your mind to ask this question cross-functionally and continually:

Value or cost? Value or cost?

57

Xerox – an idea worth copying

In an extract from the 2007 Harvard Business Review on Green Business Strategy, the following case study is cited:

> 'After nearly three decades of market dominance, Xerox found its traditional markets crowded, in the late 80s, with well funded new entrants. Their market share declined and margins eroded precipitously. In 1990, the company's executives responded with a new management initiative: the environmental leadership program – that eventually included waste reduction efforts, product 'take back' schemes and design-for-the-environment initiatives. By the mid 1990s, their large manufacturing complex in Webster NY was only sending 2% of its hazardous waste to landfills.
>
> 'Xerox's program illustrates a common pattern – dramatic cost savings are often found when a company is under tremendous pressure. As long as Xerox was the unchallenged market leader, it could afford to be easy going about cost savings – and it was. Yet when things got rough it rose to the occasion with creative initiatives.

> 'Because of the initiative, Xerox reportedly saved $50 million in its first year of the initiative. A drop in raw materials purchased was the most significant component of cost savings and fewer natural resources were used to make new machines. By 1995, Xerox estimated that it was saving more than several hundred million dollars annually by taking back used machines.
>
> 'Other manufacturers of electronic equipment such as Kodak, IBM, Canon and Hewlett Packard have also undertaken similar initiatives.'

Although 20 years have passed, the concept contained in this condensed case study of Xerox seems an idea worth copying – well before you may be forced to look at cost reduction.

58

Your cup runneth over – or run over your paper cups?

Not-for-profit organisations should, in theory, be extremely cost-conscious. A friend who works for a local church charity proudly informed me that eliminating plastic and paper cups in their head office annually saved thousands of dollars which was specifically earmarked to provide cups of soup to the homeless (yes, in recyclable paper cups).

It's not clear whether this savings took account of the water and extra time spent washing ceramic cups and mugs but apart from the preciseness of any quantified monetary savings, it still seemed a positive measure to implement, from an environmental perspective.

According to Elizabeth Rogers and Thomas M. Kostigen, co-authors of *The Green Book: The Everyday Guide to Saving the Planet One Simple Step at a Time,* Americans use more than 14 billion paper cups every year – enough to circle the world 55 times.

Isn't it worth the little extra effort to wash that ceramic cup, plate or cutlery? It might be my imagination but I swear cappuccino tastes smoother when sipped from a 'proper' cup, which seems to add to the taste and texture of the espresso experience.

59

Plastic or drastic?

Another thought on plastic ... When I first started selling customer service books and tapes at conferences (yes, tapes were a long time ago!) a customer suggested I would be offering a better service to my customers if I also provided a bag for their purchases. He outlined that they'd then wander around the conference or exhibition centre with my company name on the side of their bags so it had the added value of increasing my brand awareness. Oh yes, as it turned out, he just happened to manufacture plastic bags, on which I could have my logo printed!

It appeared to be a good idea on the surface and in burst of enthusiasm, I ordered the minimum quantity – which I believe was 10,000. The bags proved popular and I'd always casually carry anything I needed in my own branded bags. It seemed like a great suggestion by the supplier and it probably was – at the time (nearly two decades ago).

However, as the keynote speaker at the International Year of the Oceans Conference in Vancouver, along with oceanographer Jacques Cousteau, I certainly didn't unpack my plastic bags when I unpacked my bag. It suddenly dawned on me that plastic bags in an ocean or even discarded by others carelessly on a street, with my company name prominently displayed, would not only be harmful to the environment but equally harmful to my brand and my business. The bags might have initially been seen as adding value to my business but were now only adding cost – even though the cost may have long since been a hidden one.

What does one do with thousands of unused plastic bags? Throwing them out would not help the environment, since energy had already been spent in their manufacture. So it seems I have a life time supply of small plastic bags to wrap dirty shoes or washing in when I travel – thanks to that trip to the Year of the Oceans conference.

As the old proverb states:

Small drops of water make a mighty ocean ... We can all do our bit for the planet – just a tiny bit better.

60

Promotional products or landfill

I've had the privilege of addressing the Australian Promotional Products Association – and fully appreciate that strategically selected promotional products are an excellent way of promoting your organisation.

However, before you commit dollars in production costs to manufacture something with your logo that is of absolutely no value to your client base, be sure to invest some time to ensure that the product is actually aligned with your business message.

As an author who has spoken at thousands of conferences over the years, I'm dismayed at the amount of 'crap' (sorry, there is no more polite way to word this) that often clutters show bags at trade fairs-and is then thrown in the bin – attendees may discard 95% of their 'goody bag' within 24 hours.

On the other hand, I have received tastefully branded tape measures, calculators, paper weights, key rings, water bottles and mugs which have remained in my office for years after the event because they were useful and of high quality – not something tacky that would disintegrate. They weren't necessarily expensive items but products that I personally saw as adding value and every time I use them, fondly remember the company and event.

I hope that my clients do likewise if I've ever given them a shirt, calendar, luggage tag, lolly jar, mouse pad or bottle of wine that linked with a specific message or book promotion.

Of course, I always give them a personally signed copy of my books. Some clients have even used these books as giveaways to their clients or staff, whereby one of my publishers has the facility to include the client logo on the front cover and a personalised message from their CEO on the first inside pages. This makes a unique corporate gift which is usually no more costly than the price of morning tea at a major conference venue – and likely to provide attendees with 'food for thought', long after the conference ends.

My first book was on service quality and since many executive conferences were held at golf resorts, I commissioned thousands of golf tees, imprinted with QUAL-I-TEE SERVICE. It seems a little naff now but worked well at the time and I have enough golf tees to last me a lifetime. In the long-term, these inexpensive golf tees proved to be a better value proposition than the much more expensive polo shirts I also had made, as I forgot to account for the varying shapes and sizes of my diverse range of clients – and still have some unpopular sizes left.

The moral of this promotional product story is that one size doesn't fit all! It's the same principle with any value/cost comparison. Just think strategically before you spend spontaneously.

61

Lights on-but nobody home

As a child, my parents hounded me to turn off the lights whenever I left a room. As a teenager who wanted to prove a point (as teenagers do) I distinctly remember showing them some article that claimed more energy was used to actually turn lights on and off-than to leave them on continuously.

I have no idea if that was true or not in terms of lighting technology some 40 years ago, but my folks remained unconvinced and after threats of being grounded, it soon became second nature for me to always turn off the lights. It became one of my (better) lifelong habits.

Long before the days of heightened environmental awareness, I failed to convince my ex-husband of the financial merits of doing likewise. It became one of those little sources of aggravation between us (as it once had been with my parents).

Today, I have solar panels in my home but still get annoyed if anyone leaves a light on unnecessarily at home or at the office.

At least two acquaintances share this pet peeve. One was a war baby in London and has never forgotten that leaving the lights on at night increased the risk of his family home being bombed. Less drastic, another friend works in a not-for-profit organisation and had signs posted above every light switch as reminders to turn out the lights. She thinks it helped somewhat but possibly became invisible 'wallpaper' after a while.

According to a report in the *Sydney Morning Herald,* improving energy efficiency in non residential buildings consistently tops the McKinsey consulting curve and can cut emissions by 25% by 2020, at a relatively low cost of $185 per head a year to retrofit buildings (SMH March 28 2010, Paddy Manning).

I know nothing about such retro fitting and that's not within the scope of this book. However, I do know that conventional incandescent light bulbs can be replaced with compact fluorescent lights for better efficiency and cost savings.

I'm also aware that it is now common – and may soon be standard – practice in hotel rooms that guests must first place their room key card in a slot near the entrance to activate the power supply to the room. When the guest leaves the room with their key card, the lights and television automatically turn off. This is both environmentally and economically sound in terms of huge savings to the hotel on power bills.

Is there any reason this couldn't be done in public restrooms, offices and schools?

It seems that shops often have too much lighting – and energy audits actually show that the same level of brightness can usually be achieved with fewer lights, oriented differently.

When travelling in developing countries in Africa and Asia, I've noticed that many small shop owners only turn on the lights when a customer walks in. If I were a gambling person, I'd bet it's got more to do with cost than conservation.

I'm not, however, suggesting this as a strategy for your local supermarket or department store. After all, it's imperative to make premises look welcoming and safe.

However, most organisations could probably shed some generated light and make better use of natural light and natural ventilation. Could you?

62

Lights on-and everybody creative

It's not for me to comment on the success or otherwise of the controversial 2009 Copenhagen summit on climate change but I can't help but comment on what a great city it is. Cycle lanes are plentiful for commuters and even tourists can place a few kronas to hire a bicycle from a train station and then leave it at another central location and retrieve their deposit.

What's that got to do with this book? not a lot really except it puts in context a report I heard on ABC radio about the Crowne Plaza hotel which offered guests a free meal if they spent about 15 minutes on a stationary bicycle in their room to generate energy approximately 10 watts of power. Apparently, that's only about enough energy to power a couple of light bulbs but what an innovative idea (as heard on April 15 2010 on ABC 702 radio in Sydney).

A couple off days later I'm speaking at a conference at the Gold Coast, with leading lateral thinker, Dr. Edward DeBono, who's written no fewer than 80 books. He consults widely to a range of organisations and told the simple, but poignant, story of a local government council who engaged him for advice on how to reduce parking congestion. From all accounts, it was a small town with one main street and the installation and monitoring of parking meters would have proved costly.

So, what did Dr De Bono suggest?...

Allow drivers to park for as long as they liked on the main street-as long as they left their headlights on. This would allow easy access for people who wanted to do quick errands at the main shops and those who wanted to linger could simply park on one of the side streets. It seemed a solution simply brilliant in its creative simplicity.

63

Shed some light on productivity – the Hawthorne Effect

The Hawthorne Effect has been documented in many management texts throughout the years. In a nutshell, a series of experiments were conducted by Elton Mayo between 1924 and 1932 at the Hawthorne Works of the Western Electric Company near Chicago, USA.

During those studies, the intensity of light on the shop floor was varied in an effort to discover the degree of lighting that would result in the greatest productivity. Mayo found that regardless of changes in lighting, work productivity increased. Simply knowing that they were the subject of a study prompted workers to act differently. This phenomenon became known as the Hawthorne Effect.

Mayo later interviewed workers and found that supervisors tended to treat workers better during that experiment and thus, their menial task on the assembly line appeared to take on greater meaning as part of the experiment.

It seemed that changing a variable usually increased productivity, even if the variable was just a change back to the original condition. However, it is said that it is the natural process of the human being to adapt to the environment without knowing the objective of the experiment occurring.

Amongst other things, researchers hypothesised that working as a group and being treated as special were the real reasons for the productivity increase. One of Mayo's interpretations was that the individuals became a team and the team gave itself wholeheartedly and spontaneously to cooperate in the experiment.

Further interviews with the workers produced results which indicated that upward communication in an organisation can create a positive and productive work environment when workers feel that their ideas are being heard.

This Hawthorne study of nearly a century ago is still cited in management psychology today and although not *directly* related to a book on value and cost differentiation, it's a case study that has stood the test of time in regard to the importance of getting your staff involved.

What will you do to involve your staff members in regard to their suggestions about adding value or cost?

Ask them without delay – you could be 'de-lighted' with the results.

64

Techo tips

Unplug your computer and other appliances when they're not in use. You'll save money and energy.

Save: Your Money, Your time, Your Planet written by Shannon Lush and Jennifer Fleming (ABC Books, 2008) contains hints on how to save money by finding innovative uses for common household items; with such 'crafty' suggestions as recycling lampshades, melting wax ends together to make a new candle, etc.

Those authors claim that we'll rediscover the lost arts of frugality and invention and have fun in the process. Few of these money saving ideas in the home directly link to the purpose of this book – and I'd be the last person in the world to melt wax ends together. However, it was interesting and relevant to the business world that they quote Australian Choice magazine as stating that if you operate a desktop computer wireless router DVD monitor, plasma TV and DVD player on continuous standby, it could add $450 to your annual electric bill.

This principle is echoed in *The Green Book: The Everyday Guide to Saving the Planet One Simple Step at a Time* by Elizabeth Rogers and Thomas M. Kostigen. It emphatically states:

'Unplug your power. 10% of the electricity used in your home is burned by communication devices and appliances – even when they are turned off. If every US household just unplugged its computers and cell phone chargers when they were not being used, collectively we'd save over $100 million.'

I'm not sure about the precise statistics but have no doubt about the principle of unplugging unused appliances as an energy and cost saving measure. After all, the cost of energy isn't likely to be going down any day soon!

Rogers and Kostigen also claim that laptops require fewer materials and less energy to produce than desktops and use a fraction of the electricity to run: 'If you choose a laptop over a desktop, you'll save an average of 220 kilowatt-hours per year and about $20 on your annual electricity bill. If one in 23 households made its next computer purchase a laptop instead of a desktop, the energy saved could keep the lights on for every household in Silicon Valley' (page 91).

They go on to say that if you plan to upgrade your television to a flat screen (and let's face it, many businesses have televisions), you can save energy and money by purchasing an LCD screen instead of a plasma one. According to them, a 32 inch LCD panel – compared to an equal-size plasma screen – saves roughly 275 kilowatt hours of energy and $25 per year (page 93).

As for recycling old electronics, don't just throw them in the tip – look for a local electronics recycling (or should we say e-cycling) outlet.

65

Phones-get the message

Do you and your staff really need a new mobile phone every time your phone plan comes up for renewal?

Do you still need an answering machine, which uses more energy than voice mail?

For years, I paid a rather hefty monthly fee to a paging service, thinking that it seemed more professional to have a human voice answer in my absence than for a client to simply be connected to an answer machine. That was indeed a common perception, years ago, even though I was annoyed that many staff in those call centres couldn't even pronounce my name correctly, in spite of providing them with a phonetic pronunciation.

Now with voice mail on mobile, I'm readily able to update my messages on a regular basis-and can hear the message directly and accurately from the client, pick up on the intonation and never need to worry about a third party misinterpreting a message.

What's more, we can easily update and change messages to set realistic expectations of how long we may be unavailable. For example, if you're in a meeting or on a plane for X hours, simply record a greeting that let's your client know when you're next available.

I remain amazed that some plumbers and locksmiths advertise a 24-hour service but still divert callers to an answer machine message that says, 'Your call is important: please call back during normal business hours'! You could hardly consider that as adding any value.

66

Re-charge batteries and cards

Apparently if we buy rechargeable batteries, we'll also save money over the long-term.

You can also re-charge phone cards to gain savings on national and international calls. A friend had done so for many years but I resisted his suggestion as it seemed to take too much time to tediously key in the phone number for the phone card provider; then select a language; and then key in a long password before finally keying in the number of the party with whom you actually wished to speak. As if I had time to fiddle around with all that.

My friend simply set up a speed dial on my phone so I only need to key in two extra digits and, as a result, I've saved hundreds of dollars on long distance calls over the last three years. Still, with increased competition the cost of calls and bundling of telco services seems to have actually come down in real terms. This same friend who initially introduced me to the phone card (he's good on monitoring and staying up to date on these things) is now on a phone plan that gives him ample 'free' talk time for his overseas calls.

Another small business acquaintance swears by Skype and other forms of free VOIP.

Those who have their mobile phones provided by large organisations will seldom have any idea of the cost of calls or receiving downloaded data on their hand-held device – either locally or overseas. Big companies probably have amazing economies of scale with their phone plans so employees treat their phones as an extension of their lives – they're not paying the bill, after all. But do you really need to be connected 24/7? Is it wise that partners and children also use the company cell phone to make calls? Then again, is all this more costly to monitor than to pay for bulk usage?

Still, is it worth thinking about before dialling.

67

Waste-free Wednesdays – child's play

The notice board of Manly Village Public School caught my eye: 'Waste-Free Wednesdays' was all it said.

Intrigued, I called the school and spoke to deputy principal, Peta Hansen who elaborated that the program was initiated by the year-three teacher, Hannah Piper.

The aim is to encourage children to reduce the amount of landfill and encourage healthy eating by bringing package free lunches that can be recycled or composted. Students are encouraged to use reusable containers and re-sealable plastic bags.

The school offers packaging tips to parents in the newsletter and gives stickers and certificates to motivate the students.

There was an apparent reduction from 35.2 grams of packaging per child to 2.2 grams per child. OK, it's not exactly a cost saving tip for the school but still worth mentioning because it began as a once off competition, then a monthly event and now is fixed as Waste-Free Wednesdays.

Could your organisation devise your own version of Waste-Free Wednesdays – or Waste-Free Weeks –

all small steps to a Waste-Free World? OK, that might never happen, but isn't it worth aspiring to?

I'm delighted to learn that a zoo employee suggested that animal waste be recycled and sold to garden shops as a unique range of fertiliser. You've just gotta love that innovative concept of 'Zoo pooh'!

68

Wasted space at your place

Having once been a teacher myself, I was reminded of how many school buildings previously sat completely idle outside of normal school hours. What a waste of space and potential revenue. This has improved over the years with many premises now sub-let after hours to adult education classes.

Some schools subsidise their operating costs by renting out sports fields for community events or weekend markets – or even as car spaces if parking is at a premium in the area at certain hours or for special community events.

A psychologist in our office block works nine-to-five and has her rent subsidised by a masseur who treats clients in the evenings and on weekends.

Of course there are insurance and security risks to consider, but can you gain any additional revenue from wasted space at your place?

69

National leftovers day-a recipe for success?

The inaugural National Leftovers Day was launched on December 26, 2009 by Jon Dee and a company called Foodwise. If at first, you don't see the relevance to business, be sure to read to the end of this chapter...

The goal of National Leftovers Day is to reduce food waste and its environmental and financial costs. Boxing Day was the ideal time to do so. Food waste peaks in the festive season when, according to 2008 figures, Australians spent $7.6 billion on food in December alone. In 2009, Food Wise commissioned national research on our attitudes to food waste. 60% of Australians admitted they wasted even more food than usual at Christmas time. The average New South Wales household throws out about $643 worth of food per year! Survey participants did not know that food rotting in landfill gave off methane 20 times more potent than car exhaust pollution. By being a bit more careful with our food, we can really save money and the environment.

The author of the Australia Institute's 'What a Waste' report said that the $5.2 billion spent on food that was thrown out was enough to meet the financial shortfall in the United Nations emergency relief fund and more than the amount Australians spent on digital equipment in 2007.

An article appearing in the Manly Daily states: 'An analysis of the latest figures indicates that Australians throw out three million tonnes of food waste every year. That's equivalent to 145 kilograms of food waste for each Australian. Australians are now spending five billion dollars a year on food that we buy but don't eat.

'Some experts believe that we're throwing away at least 20% of the food we buy. That's the equivalent of buying five bags of groceries and throwing one away. Given the cost of today's food, that's clearly not sustainable for the family budget.'

You may well ask if such waste is sustainable in any budget – whether household, government or big or small business?

'Muda' is a traditional Japanese term for an activity that is wasteful and doesn't add value or is un-productive. My local sushi shop insists on automatically giving a little plastic container of soy sauce even when I specifically say I don't need it. And, I only need one of those little satchels of salt for my take away chips. On the other hand, a friend in advertising tells me that a leading household brand name of mustard claims that their profit is what the consumer leaves on their plate! How often do we receive – or use – more condiments than what we actually need?

Spice things up a bit. What about declaring and dedicating a day – or even half a day – to focus on workplace waste awareness?

It doesn't need to be a national campaign – simply set aside time from everyday operations to have laser sharp focus on 'leftovers' and potential waste in your own organisation.

Make it fun and offer incentives to employees and/or teams who come up with viable suggestions.

National Leftovers Day ran a competition to share the best Christmas-themed leftover recipes that would inspire others to get food wise on Boxing Day.

Why not be an innovative business and cook up your own recipe for success to reduce waste in your workplace? One embryonic idea implemented today could whet your appetite for further innovative savings. You don't need to be a master chef or a master strategist to taste the fruits of frugality.

70

Mouth-watering savings

Speaking of taste, it's hard to beat the flavour of mouth-watering potato chips, but until reading an article in a Qantas in flight magazine, I had no idea how much water was actually used to produce these savoury snacks.

Smith's Snack foods, in South Australia, recognised water as a diminishing resource worldwide and looked at what it could do to reduce vast quantities of water used in production. 'In 1997 it was using 315 million litres a year, mostly washing potatoes. For about $65,000, a waste water treatment plant was installed to allow most of the water to be recycled. It took just five weeks before the outlay was recouped. The company is now saving over $130,000 annually on its water bill with plans to further reduce the amount of water needed.'

Can you recycle water, even on a smaller scale?

Although it's a treat I only allow myself to indulge in occasionally, there's nothing quite like an ice cold Coke to accompany that pack of chips. Coca Cola now studies the linkages between climate change and water availability and how this will impact the location of its new bottling facilities (*Harvard Business Review on Green Business Strategy* – 2007, Kimberly O'Neill Packard & Forest L Reinhardt).

Water is indeed our most precious natural resource. Humans can survive without food for long periods of time – but not without water. This may be commonly accepted in theory but, frankly, I don't believe we can ever fully appreciate how important water is until we have had to go without it.

Yes, we are sympathetic to reports of drought and famine in Africa or drought and loss of livestock closer to home, but it wasn't until 23 years ago, when my throat was parched in the middle of the Thar Desert near the border of India and Pakistan, that I truly felt (not just intellectualised – but truly felt) the priceless value of water. Riding on camels we had severe water rations placed on our own water supplies. We were en route to the town of Jaiselmeer, which was once the major hub of the trade routes of old – an oasis in the middle of the desert which once held a big lake. On that day, there was no such lake. It had dried up and four year-old children had never seen rain!

That was probably the turning point my life: when I realised I was a closet 'greenie'. never again would I brush my teeth with the tap running. Never again would I shower without a bucket to capture some of the run off to water the plants. I even became more aware about water wasted with each flush of the toilet and adopted the practice of: 'If it's yellow, let it mellow. If it's brown, flush it down.' Admittedly, a couple of friends found this practice somewhat disgusting so I only do so when I'm the only one in the house!

Nearly 20 years later, I read that: 'If we flushed just one less time per day, we'd save about 4.5 gallons of water – as much water as the average person in Africa uses for a whole day of drinking, cooking, bathing and cleansing. By 2025, the world must increase its water supply by 22% in order to meet its needs. Meanwhile, 40% of the drinking water supplied to homes is flushed down the toilet.' (*The Green Book: The Everyday Guide to Saving the Planet One Simple Step at a Time,* Elizabeth Rogers and Thomas M. Kostigen)

For hygiene reasons, it's not suggested that you don't flush in the workplace but certainly think about it if you're a home-based business – and you're not flush with funds. I have no idea what the cost savings are but know there would certainly be some – and increasingly, homes (including my own) now use only rain water – not mains water – for the toilets and garden.

Small businesses often have bigger hot water systems than they need. If your premises have gardens, use drip irrigation or soaker hoses instead of regular sprinklers.

71

To wash or not to wash? that is the question

Do you really need filtered water delivered to the office? Is it really better for us, health-wise, or just trendy? The jury is divided on this one but tap water is fine by me in first world countries. And if you insist on filtered water, it's pretty easy to buy an economical portable and reusable water filter.

Why not wash and refill water bottles when you go to work, the gym or travel? even though liquid is still sometimes confiscated at airport security checks, you can still take the empty bottle through and fill it up with water from the tap or fountain on the other side, saving the cost of purchasing a new bottle at inflated airport prices. When I mentioned this to one of my rather affluent corporate clients, who flies at least four times a week, she estimated that she saved at least three dollars per flight, four flights per week, 48 weeks per year for an annual average savings of $576! She claims this money is now used to buy duty free champagne-gotta love that logic!

Yes, re-using water bottles is also good for the environment. Manly Council, centre of a major tourist destination, even has an arrangement with a leading filtered water company to provide free filtered water along the beach front and main shopping area – in an attempt to discourage tourists from simply chucking their empty plastic bottles into the ocean.

Think about how things used to be. Here are some facts about the 1500s, where recycling water seemed taken to the extreme:

Most people got married in June, because they took their yearly bath in May and still smelled pretty good by June. However, since they were starting to pong a bit, brides carried a bouquet of flowers, to hide the body odour. Hence, the custom of carrying a bouquet.

Baths consisted of a big tub filled with hot water. The man of the house had the privilege of the nice clean water, followed by the sons. The women were next and finally the children. Lastly, the babies were washed. By then the water was so dirty you could actually lose a small object in it. Thus, the saying, 'Don't throw the baby out with the bath water'

72

Clean cars

It's not the purpose of this book to debate the pros and cons of whether the best form of transport is walking, cycling, riding a scooter, driving a car or taking public transport. As a keen cyclist, I have a slight bias, but cars do indeed have an important place in our world. Since we were discussing water in the last chapter, let's first look at the value/cost equation of washing the car.

There are claims that washing your car in a commercial car wash, that uses recycled water, is better for the environment than doing it yourself and there are also waterless car wash products on the market. So which is best and most cost effective?

Again, **ID** – **I**t **D**epends. Identify the opportunity cost of doing it yourself, hiring a neighbourhood kid or having it cleaned professionally. Of course, this also probably is dictated by how car-proud you may – or may not – be.

I occasionally wash mine with a sponge and water from the rainwater tank but more often than not, I have it professionally cleaned when I leave it in the airport parking station. I simply see my car as a means of transport. I don't use it for clients and it's not an extension of my ego so I feel time spent cleaning could be invested more productively on other pursuits.

In this instance, I'm more time-sensitive than cost-sensitive and, the guys at the airport clean cars every day and do a better job than I could; plus they get the grime off from the undercarriage with their mechanised brushes, which in theory will reduce rust and add longer term value to my vehicle. It's also extremely time-efficient since I'm already at the location and don't have to wait 20 minutes over a 'free' cup of poor quality coffee to have it cleaned at a local commercial outlet.

Now, in case you're thinking that airport parking is expensive, you're absolutely right. So, if I'm gone for more than a few days, it's more economical and slightly faster (using transit lanes) to take a taxi. The breakeven point works out at four days. If I have no luggage or deadline, I use public transport. There's that opportunity cost concept again. What's yours?

73

Car-less or careless

It's funny how my attitude towards transport has changed over the years. I couldn't wait to get a shiny new bicycle when I was eight years old but saw that more as a form of fun than a form of transport.

My parents didn't own a car so my big goal (make that obsession) as a teenager was to buy a car just as soon as I was old enough to get my licence. It was a feeling of freedom and independence and I prized my little green, slightly dented, second hand, gas-guzzling car; as I never again had to wait in blizzards for the bus to arrive. Thus started a lifelong journey as 'the car' became my major transport, until...

IBM posted me to Japan in 1986. Individuals could not own a car unless they owned a parking spot, which were as scarce as hen's teeth. So I took the train and bought a scooter to whiz around Tokyo traffic – there was little point having a car when I couldn't understand the street signs anyway.

Back in Australia, IBM provided me with an ever impressive range of company cars – the bigger the car, the better the promotion – and I never thought twice about the cost of servicing them, nor depreciation, until I started my own business and was faced with a huge capital cost – not to mention registration, insurance and maintenance. Should I buy or lease?

(That's a tax question for the accountants – and more later on leasing or buying equipment and premises.)

After my business was well-established, I bought a Mercedes sports car which, to a kid from the 'wrong side of the tracks', seemed pretty sensational. Ironically, it also seemed somewhat excessive and egotistical, so felt I had to justify this purchase by emphasising that it was 'only' second-hand. I really shouldn't have felt the need to do so but for some reason, I did.

After all, I'd read in the new York Times best seller, *The Millionaire Next Door,* that millionaires in the United States do not always live in expensive neighbourhoods, wear designer suits or drive flash cars. The research indicated that the majority of millionaires lived well below their means and that only 23.5% of millionaires surveyed owned a new car. Most of them bought demo or low mileage second hand cars, since motor vehicles depreciate the moment they leave showroom.

I also justified that the Merc was one of the safest vehicles on the road and happily drove it for eight years, even though my accountant told me I'd be better off financially if I took taxis. Still, as already confessed, a car was my way of life. I was even silly enough (in hindsight) to often spend one and a half hours driving into the city in rush hour and pay $90 per day to park it. It was simply my modus operandi – and not a very clever one at that.

One day, as I rushed out the door, complaining about the traffic, I bumped into my elderly neighbour. She questioned: 'Why don't you take the ferry?' I looked at her and wondered what she would know about work pressures? However, as I drove off, the radio announced that there was an accident on the Sydney Harbour Bridge, which meant I'd never reach my destination in time anyway, so I thought I might as well try the ferry. I have to admit that I had no idea of the timetable, cost or even where to buy a ticket; but figured it must run frequently so re-parked the car at home and headed down to the terminal.

Much to my delight, I arrived in the city half an hour later and walked a few short blocks to my destination. Not only did I save money on parking, but magnificent harbour views reduced my stress levels. And, I could use that half hour trip to read, rather than sit in traffic. Since then, I could probably count on my fingers the number of times I drive the car to the city, unless of course, I have boxes of books to take to a conference.

My accountant noted the reduced car usage and suggested (shock horror) that it really wasn't economical for me to maintain an expensive car. He produced a spreadsheet to show actual savings even if I took taxis. Well, he was probably right, but the car was convenient and had nothing owing on it, so I saw no need to change until...

The registration came due two days before I was heading overseas for an extended time frame. When I took the car for what I expected would be a quick standard safety check, the mechanic informed me that it required new brake pads, which couldn't be done before my flight. As I had been thinking of upgrading anyway, I sold it virtually on the spot.

I declared that I was going to be more environmentally conscious and do without a car on a trial basis. A friend questioned my decision and bet that I wouldn't last more than six months. I readily accepted that wager because I would be overseas for three of those months anyway. How hard could it be to go without a car for another three months?

It was around the same time that Al Gore released the popular environmental documentary, *An Inconvenient Truth.* I was no doubt partially influenced by his arguments for greater environmental responsibility but found the film was aptly named because, to tell the truth, it was somewhat of an inconvenience to go without a car, initially. I'd long since sussed the ferry schedule but had never been on a local bus, so I faced a bit of a learning curve. Still, I reasoned, I'd always used public transport in London, Tokyo, new York and Paris – why not Sydney? Well, I was usually in holiday mode in those places with more discretionary time and had 'always' had a car in Australia.

Waiting at a bus stop one rainy morning, I questioned the wisdom of my commitment to be car-less for six months, but after a few weeks I slipped into a different routine and changed my mindset.

To prove a point, I extended the bet – double or nothing – to go without a car for an entire year. As circumstances eventuated, I didn't own a car for over three and a half years, as I seldom needed one for work. I was lucky that my best friend and her boyfriend, who lived nearby, owned two cars for work but only needed one for weekends, so we came to a win/win arrangement where I filled their tank every weekend in exchange for occasional use of the car.

Car-less or careless? Having not owned a car for nearly four years, would it be environmentally irresponsible to buy another?

After all, during the first year of not owning a car, my accountant calculated that even with increased taxi use, I had actually saved

Nearly $2400, which was donated to buy donkeys and water purification units for third world countries (and, that didn't even account for depreciation). nearing the completion of building my own home, it simply wasn't practical to get to and from hardware stores without a vehicle, in which to cart bulky samples of paint, timber and tiles; and I felt no guilt whatsoever purchasing a (fuel-efficient) car again.

At one stage, an expensive car had added more cost than real value to my life. Yet I still placed an emotional value on driving in a luxury vehicle and I may well buy another one – certainly not as an investment but as a lifestyle choice.

A friend has five cars, three of which are vintage models and are probably worth more than he paid for them since he meticulously restored them as a hobby.

Most of us have more transport choices than we think. But let's at least think about the value or cost (real or emotional) of that choice.

74

Rental cars

Rental car companies charge a huge premium for petrol if you return the car without a full fuel tank. It's sometimes double the amount of the going rate at the bowsers and I often wondered why anyone wouldn't fill up beforehand?

Admittedly, there are times when we may be running late to catch a flight and/or don't pass a nearby service station. However, the main reason is because most rentals are corporate rentals and the driver isn't actually paying the bill! Yes, the employee's time is valuable but so too is the time of a business owner and most owners (including many wealthy ones) wouldn't think twice to take five minutes at the pump to save well over $50 of pre-tax money.

Here's a hint whereby rental car companies could spend just a minute to add value to frequent drivers in their loyalty programs. Have you ever got into a car in a strange city and fiddled for ages with the radio to find a station that suits your musical or news taste? It seems the frequency is always pre-set at 100 decibels (OK, I'm exaggerating) to the musical inclinations of the 20 year old who last cleaned the vehicle. How easy would it be for the rental car company to include in a frequent driver profile, a customer's nominated preferences for music or news?

It would be very little cost in terms of time to set the stations but added value to the driver, who would then feel the car rental company is literally 'tuned into' the wants of the customer.

75

Cost drivers

If employees use their own vehicles, are they reimbursed for motor vehicle travel at the Australian Tax Office or Internal Revenue Service mileage rates? It may be worth looking at whether it's cheaper to rent a vehicle? On several recent trips of several hundred miles, the rental car method saved one employer more than 50% of the cost of reimbursing the employee for personal mileage.

Of course, there may not be a rental car company conveniently located – so you have the extra opportunity cost of the employee's time to get there. Then again, they may be just around the corner or offer free delivery to your pick up point.

Do you truly understand what's really driving costs in your organisation?

76

Drive costs down to deliver the goods

Traffic is a nightmare in most large cities. If you make your own deliveries, spend a bit of time in advance planning efficient routes so you don't waste time and fuel zig-zagging across town. It seems so obvious but you'd be surprised at the propensity to just hop in the car, truck or van with only a rough idea of your route. Take a few minutes in advance to look at a map or GPS.

Use off-peak times to drive if viable. Otherwise plan your route, if possible, to go against the main flow of rush hour traffic. It's probably also possible to cut the frequency of non-essential deliveries to decrease those fuel expenses.

77

Energy audits – better utilise utilites

Consider contacting your electric, gas and water suppliers to ask whether they offer energy audits. Ask whether you qualify for an off-peak rate plan. Ask for recommendations on energy conservation tools. Something as simple as cleaning filters on a washing machine and regular servicing can also yield savings.

It might be time to look at the payback time for new heating and cooling units – and the utility companies and/or government may even offer incentives to help you pay for some of them.

78

Turn up the heat to reduce heating costs

Is it possible and practical to set your thermostat just one degree higher for air-conditioning and one degree lower for heating? Doing so could save a small or home-based business hundreds of dollars per year on their utility bill. Of course, the larger the premises, the larger the savings you stand to make, while still being sure to provide a comfortable work environment for all employees and customers.

As the owner of my local photo shop points out, many Australian retail businesses leave entrance doors wide open to appear more welcoming to passing trade. They also leave air conditioning and heating running on full blast – much of it escaping through the open door. Not my local photographer, Harvey Gordon. He sees the bigger picture and figures that any customer who may be intimidated by the closed door is more than compensated for through *definite* significant energy savings. Of course, he has a prominent sign on the clear glass door, saying 'Welcome – We're Open.'

Be open to examining all costs under the lens. If you only operate Monday to Friday, with no perishable goods, do you need the heating and air conditioning running over the weekend at full strength, at partial output or not at all?

Likewise, is it viable to close the curtains when it's sunny in the summer and when it's cold in the winter? This could reduce energy needs by up to 25%. According to Rogers and Kostigen: 'If every house in America kept the curtains closed for additional insulation, the total energy saved annually would be as much as the entire nation of Japan uses in a year' (*The Green Book: The Everyday Guide to Saving the Planet One Simple Step at a Time* Elizabeth Rogers and Thomas M. Kostigen).

Of course, you wouldn't have curtains closed in areas with customer traffic, nor would you want your staff members to feel they were operating like underground moles. Common sense should always prevail.

Insulate roofs, doors and windows with safe materials and weather stripping. Again, you'd find annual savings that would exceed your initial cost outlay.

Speaking of stripping, it's hard to make this stuff sexy! But, green can, at least, be cool...

79

Green is the new black

Green is indeed cool. Green is the new black. Just ask Scott Kilmartin, who won the City of Melbourne Business of the Year Award. Founder of Haul.com.au , he created a brand of cool street wear and bags made from rubbish that is both funky and eco-friendly, through recycling materials such as old inner tubes and licence plates.

Most of us think of billboards as being made of paper but Scott discovered that they were made of vinyl so recycles them into laptop bags and dog collars.

He turned trash to cash and created a cool new brand in the process.

I'm probably too old to be considered 'cool', but as a keen cyclist, I now at least sport a rather hip-looking inner tube to keep my jeans from sagging down around my hips.

80

Green is good-simple is sensational

Forget the 90s, when some fictitious Wall Street movie character proclaimed that greed was good. now green is good.

Kimberly O'neill Packard and Forest L Reinhardt state in the 2007 Harvard Business Review:

'We know of companies that began by conducting a carbon audit to uncover inefficient and costly energy practices and then moved on to identify opportunities for brand enhancement around the issue of climate change.'

Apparently, going above and beyond the call of regulatory duty is a way to gain respect.

'Natural capitalism seeks to not only reduce waste but to eliminate the very concept of waste. In closed loop production systems, modelled on nature's designs, every output either is returned harmlessly to the ecosystem as a nutrient or compost or becomes an input for manufacturing another product.'

They conclude 'This whole system thinking can help managers find small changes that lead to big savings that are cheap, free or even better than free (because they make whole systems cheaper to build).'

81

Transparent thoughts on anti-oxidants

Pears soap, invented in 1789, is the world's oldest soap brand. Its unique manufacturing process required the soap be dried for up to 13 weeks in order for the alcohol used in the process to evaporate (and be re-used)

The bars were laid out on wooden trays in huge drying rooms. The trays are stacked vertically so that the soap in the top trays is exposed to a hotter air than those on the lower trays and becomes much darker, almost black sometimes.

Unilever, the marketing company, were keen to be able to exploit the transparency of the soap, but this was difficult given that some of the bars were totally opaque. The solutions were relatively simple:

- after six or seven weeks rotate the trays so that those at the top were moved to the bottom
- employ large paddle wheels so that the air circulated better and a uniform temperature throughout the drying rooms could be achieved
- totally re-duct the way in which the hot air entered the drying rooms to achieve the same effect

But all these cost much more money than the brand could afford. In 1971, the agency team from the Pears soap advertising agency, Foote Cone and Belding (FCB) visited the Pears soap factory in Port Sunlight-to get a better understanding of how the soap was made, in the hope this might provide some insight for their next advertising campaign.

It so happened that the agency team sat in on the meeting, albeit at the back of the room with the expectation that they took no part.

During the meeting the factory team explained once again the problem and the solution to stop bars becoming black. It was simply a question of money, and unaffordable.

However, the agency account director, unusually, had read chemistry at Cambridge University. Sitting in the meeting he considered the problem from another point of view. not how to stop the bars getting too hot, but why it was, when they got hot, did they turn black. He suggested that the darkening was caused by an oxidation problem

Somewhat hesitantly, with an astounded marketing department and deeply suspicious factory team present, he outlined his thinking and suggested they simply add an anti-oxidant to the mix.

Three months later trials with the antioxidant proved totally successful. At minimum cost the problem was overcome. This in fact allowed not only different coloured transparent Pears soap to be produced, but also Pears shampoo.

The moral of this story is that looking at cost problem, however old and seemingly insoluble, through a different set of eyes may produce unexpected results.

Richard Oldcorn was that advertising executive and although the example is almost 40 years old, the principal is just as relevant today.

82

Re-use solvents to stay solvent

It took the Wattyl paint factory in Australia just one year to recoup the $100,000 spent on a distillation unit that recovers solvent used in cleaning tanks and equipment. Now instead of paying someone to dispose of the solvents, the company now recovers up to 90% of the solvents and uses them again.

It also recovers up to 60% of previously wasted paint and a whole new product. a primer, has been created from the final distillery sludge (according to a 2009 edition of Qantas magazine.)

Not all of us may have need for a distillation unit in our plant or office but we can all examine our equivalent of 'sludge' to see if there are any opportunities amidst a mire of what is currently seen as waste.

83

Green outcomes – and red paperclips

Even if they're not looking for greener outcomes, savvy manufacturing executives should always ask what can be done to increase overall efficiency of production. Can this be achieved through reduced fixed overheads? Should you consider new suppliers or encourage existing ones to lower costs? Or find a more competitive supply chain? Or even use a barter system?

Kyle MacDonald, a young man in Canada, actually traded a paperclip for a house! He started with one red paperclip on July 12, 2005 and one year and 14 trades later, he traded with the town of Kipling, Saskatchewan, for a house located at 503 Main Street. *One Red Paperclip: Or How an Ordinary Man Achieved His Dream with the Help of a Simple Office Supply* went on to become a best seller.

84

True green – sweat the small stuff

A friend's daughter was pursuing a Masters degree in environmental law. She's a bright, personable young woman and I enjoy listening to – but not always agreeing with – her perspective. In the midst of sometimes heated debates with her father, I would quietly admire her stance and passion to make the world a more ecologically sustainable place.

She would have facts and figures readily available to support her argument and would seldom concede a single point of compromise. She'll no doubt be an excellent lawyer once she recognises the need to sometimes compromise.

However, when she moved to a new flat, her mother discovered a bunch of fully functional highlighters, markers, pens and pencils thrown in the bin, worth approximately $50. It seemed especially wasteful for a still-struggling student; it was also an ironic double standard for someone so committed to the environment to still have such a casual attitude to that throw-away mentality.

Sometimes we get so carried away looking at the big theoretical picture that we overlook the little practical applications.

And yes, I believe her mother is still using some of those writing implements!

85

Purchase in bulk – but baulk before over-committing

Consider discounts on the purchase of bulk quantities.

Ink in pens will dry up faster than lead in pencils! If past experience shows that the product can be used or sold within a reasonable time frame, take advantage of the price difference. This will result in higher profits and less money spent in the long run.

However, make sure to look before you leap and don't automatically shift to bulk purchases, because oversupply or waste will only result in dead inventory. Be sure to consider the storage costs associated with increased inventory and whether the products are perishable.

A factory manager may choose to occasionally order huge quantities of parts, which reduces the order cost but maximises the carrying cost. Otherwise they may order frequently to reduce carrying cost but maximise ordering cost. The least total cost is the inventory level when both ordering and carrying costs are minimised.

A friend's husband has their garage full of 'deals' he got on building materials that he hasn't touched in over 15 years. Meanwhile, she parks her car outside on the frosty streets of Canada – where it is subject to more wear and tear than any potential savings from the 'useless inventory' snugly stored in their garage.

Admittedly, I can be a bit of a hoarder. For example, I always seemed to have a ready supply of small, clean cardboard boxes, which when emptied of books, could be readily reused. In fact, I swear some of these must have bred in my garage. I had plenty of space at the time so there was no need to cull and there was always ample to give to friends who were moving house (remember, removalists charge you for boxes). However, when it came time for me to move house and store my full boxes of books in self storage, it was no longer viable to pay for storage space for a bunch of empty boxes. If, by chance, I needed one – I'd now just buy it at the post office.

86

Lease or buy?

Although my personal preference is to purchase most capital goods outright, I know that this isn't always possible – nor is it necessarily the most financially prudent course of action.

Most of us borrow to buy a home and there are indeed advantages to using 'other people's' money and what economists would label 'good debt'.

I'm neither an economist, financier or accountant and don't intend to advise on such matters but I would caution that you always seek a *complete* analysis of the pros and cons of leasing versus purchasing, because there are often hidden costs in the former. There are also advantages depending on your business model and tax position, both of which are variable.

Premises are the most commonly leased item and it certainly makes sense for any start-up business to lease – just in case they've misjudged their market or their ideal location. And let's face it – unless you've won the lottery or inherited a small fortune from Uncle Fred, it's not even an option to consider the purchase of premises.

However, down the track it may prove advantageous to place a deposit on premises and put the rent money towards the mortgage. Of course there are all sorts of complex tax structures (which constantly change) on possibly buying the premises in your super fund or family trust.

If you lease your facility, take a look at the terms and conditions around rent increases in your lease. Many commercial leases calculate rent increases using the CPI (Consumer Price Index). If your lease contains such CPI adjustments, you may want to negotiate a modest cap over the previous year to protect you from unexpected large increases if inflation is rampant.

If it is time to replace computers or other technology, look carefully at a lease versus buy analysis. Technology changes so rapidly that leasing may be the more cost effective alternative. Be sure to carefully weigh up any savings against any projected performance outcomes and your taxable income.

Most large organisations use fleet rental companies to supply for cars and trucks, without the worry of ongoing maintenance. Individuals can likewise lease or buy motor vehicles. Again, think **ID: I**t **D**epends on cash flow, office, mileage driven and your tax situation. I can't recall the exact circumstances but at one stage, my accountant advised me to lease a car and at another time, he recommended outright purchase.

It's a good investment to get good advice. There's no point paying over-the-top for a good or service that you don't really need – just to get a tax break! I once received a humorous Christmas card from my accountant with a jolly picture of Santa, saying: 'May you pay lots of tax next year' At a glance it seemed rather odd, as surely we all want to pay minimal tax? But, of course, it implied that it's better to make a healthy profit and pay tax – than to make a loss and pay none!

87

Credit card confusion

Again, I'm not a financial planner and it's not my role to advise but I can't help but urge you in the strongest possible terms to think twice – or three, four or five times – before continually racking up uncontrolled or unnecessary expenses on your credit card.

I use both my company and personal credit cards regularly. They are convenient and provide a ready record of expenses and save time with auto debit from trusted suppliers (e.g. health fund, water board). I may even get frequent flier points and while using credit card company funds, my own money is in the bank gaining interest for another 30 days.

I'm one of these boring people who pays off the entire amount owing each month so I am not a very profitable customer for the credit card companies.

I understand the concept of compound interest and having once worked for the Department of Consumer Affairs, have witnessed the devastation to many businesses and families as their debt continues to spiral out of control.

Using other people's money can be a good strategy but only adds more and more cost when you get deeper and deeper into debt.

It may not always be possible to pay off the entire amount during a cash flow crisis, but always try to pay off as much as you can afford to – not just the minimal required. In the days before electronic statements and banking, I was overseas for two months and had left signed, blank cheques for my PA to pay my credit card bill when it arrived. She dutifully did so but only paid the minimal amount required. Since my airfares had been purchased on credit, the interest was outrageous and I was outraged – until I sadly realised that was her modus operandi.

She'd often joke: 'When things get drastic, put it on plastic.' But it was no joke that no one had ever explained compound interest to her and she was in a constant cycle of debt. When she later received a Christmas bonus, I suggested that would help towards paying off some of her debt – and was sad to see her spend the entire amount on junky toys for her unappreciative nieces and nephews.

I realise I said I didn't mean to give advice but I simply couldn't help myself as crippling credit card debt only adds cost to your business – and your life.

88

Make invisible costs visible

In T *he Power to Change Anything* (McGraw Hill – 2007), Kerry Patterson encourages organisations to make the invisible visible. 'Place the price of hospital equipment where it can be seen by practitioners.'

Likewise, why not post the cost of a broken wine glass on the door of commercial kitchen? Or the cost to throw out a well-done steak that has been returned, when the customer asked for it rare? It can never be reused. What about the cost of toner, or paper, displayed above the photo copier (which always seems to have an overflowing garbage bin next to it)?

There is so much money in organisations that employees don't think about – not because they're bad people but because it simply doesn't register on their radar. Most office workers wouldn't have a clue about the cost of toner cartridges, pens, broken chairs, monthly phone bills or computer repairs. Make such invisible costs more visible.

Have costs of those most frequently wasted raw materials highly visible to factory workers. There are no guarantees, unless staff members are held personally responsible for the cost of any wastage (which I'm not suggesting), but they're likely to at least be somewhat more careful if they know that a commonly used ingredient costs $200 per litre, rather than three dollars per litre. Otherwise, who’s to know?

89

Sack 'em or save 'em?

Are employees your most valuable asset or a costly liability? It may be a question whether staff members add value or cost to the bottom line? It's always a temptation for across-the-board staff cuts to be the first cost-saving option in any economic downturn.

Think carefully before letting good performers go during tough times. Conversely, think about the cost of keeping poor performers on the payroll in good times.

In *Good to Great* (Harper Collins 2001), best-selling author Jim Collins challenges the old adage that people are your most important asset. He clarifies: 'People are not your most important asset – the right people are your most important asset.'

In a survey of 1,435 Fortune 500 companies, his team of researchers found that:

'Leaders get the right people on the bus, the wrong people off. They get the right people in the right seat – and then they figured out where to drive it.'

Do you have the right people on your bus? Are you heading in the right direction? Or are you about to drive over a cliff?

It's a reasonably safe bet that any organisation with more than 20 people probably has a few that aren't pulling their weight. Yet, we keep them on the payroll for fear of industrial action or because we 'like' them (or maybe even love them if it's a family business). It may be because we think it's a case of better the devil we know than the devil we don't. Or perhaps we just don't want to face up to an unpleasant task and live in hope that they might change.

By all means, offer marginal performers every opportunity to change. Outline specific issues in regular performance reviews and coach them on areas that need improvement. Clearly outline, verbally and in writing, aspects that need to be adjusted. However, you need to admit that sometimes it's easier to change people – than to change people! Some people just won't change and you don't need them on your bus.

Stop procrastinating and remove poor quality staff members who aren't adding value. In fact, they have the extra cost in that it's de-motivating for your good staff to carry the extra load. Firing someone is never an easy or pleasant task but consider 'freeing up their future' to save a heap of money for the future benefit of every employee in your organisation.

Those – often wasted – wages could be used to hire better suited staff and/or invested to further improve the skill set of your existing team.

Even in a downturn, think twice – or three or four times – before you let a good long-term employee go. Remember, you will have the hidden costs of re-training someone else-without a track record when business picks up again.

90

Staff training

'An investment in knowledge pays the best dividends' – Benjamin Franklin

Is training an investment in human capital? Is it one of the first budget items cut during tough times? Or could there be a possible educational upside to an economic downturn?

Employee training can indeed cost a lot of money. not training employees can cost even more.

Are you maximising the use of your physical plant and equipment – or do you have the equivalent of a Rolls Royce that employees only know how to drive as a beat up used car? Are they up to speed with the latest regulations and legislation in your industry that could avoid costly legal suits? There may even be a fatal accident if safety standards slip. Are they intellectually stimulated and feel valued in an atmosphere that encourages learning? What if they get bored and join a competitor who offers more opportunities for self-improvement?

Of course, it's ridiculous to enrol in every training program that passes your desk and important to strike the right balance without putting a big strike through the entire training budget.

Even a downturn may prove a good time to have your workforce sharpen their skills. There's the old story of two woodsmen in the wilds of northern Canada. One lumberjack was bigger and stronger and worked at a furious pace, seldom taking a break. The smaller man consistently chopped more timber during a day and took frequent breaks to rest from the heavy strenuous labour to regularly sharpen his axe and thus increase his productivity.

Find the right balance between working smarter – not just harder – and sharpen the proverbial axe in your organisation. Better that than axing staff or training programs in a haphazard manner.

If you simply treat people like numbers, you likely won't make your numbers. This applies to large and small organisations alike.

Tom O'Toole, owner of a prosperous bakery in Beechworth, a small country town in Victoria, is often asked how he can afford to train his staff:

'What if you train 'em and they leave?' ask other small business owners in the town.

'Yeah,' replies Tom dryly, 'but what if I don't train 'em and they stay!'

91

Staff rewards

If we expect employees to think of it as their business in terms of saving cost and adding value, they must also be rewarded in terms of reaping a percentage of additional profits.

This is not about sophisticated remuneration, bonus and benefit schemes (though these are important and some organisations have entire teams of people dedicated to developing these). It's not about employee of the month programs or other forms of public celebration of excellence.

In the 2009 launch issue of 'Speaker Station – Leaders and Professional Walk Your Talk' magazine, Michael Podolinsky cites an example of the value of involving employees in the cost-cutting profit enrichment process.

'Ask them where savings could come from and then give them a bonus based on the percentage of whatever the organisation saves over the first year. A friend of mine at Unisys had this offered to him. He noticed wood pallets stacking up in the back. He made six phone calls and found a company that would pay 50 cents more per pallet than the previous company to collect them – which saved Unisys $50,000 per year. He received a $5,000 bonus cheque which motivated him and a dozen other employees at that location to start looking for more cost saving and money producing measures.'

One could argue that the best incentive for staff members to be actively involved is that they get to keep their job! But let's be realistic. A simple tangible reward, visibly linked to any potential savings, will serve as a greater incentive for staff to give a bit of extra thought to add value and reduce cost.

92

Re-charge your own battery

We spoke earlier about re-charging batteries and phone cards for potential cost savings.

Let's now briefly consider the enormous long-term costs if you don't re-charge your own battery.

When I worked in Japan 20 years ago, I was amazed that 12-14 hour days, six days a week, were the norm for most salaried office workers then. Were those hours actually spent adding extra value to the organisation? I initially struggled to keep up the pace to prove that I wasn't a 'lazy Westerner' until I realised that most staff members stayed out of a sense of obligation in a culture where no one went home before the boss. Some would actually nod off at their desk. This added questionable value to the organisation and was a huge 'cost' to many individuals. After a brief stint in hospital with pneumonia (partially brought on by sheer exhaustion), I decided that enough was enough and insisted my team leave the office by 8pm – convinced that fewer hours equalled more productivity.

An over whelming workload can be a trap for business owners who often feel they can't 'afford' to take time off. These are usually dynamic individuals with a total commitment to achieve their goals and may appear to the outside world as supermen or superwomen. But what cost to their business if their immune system gets so run down that they end up hospital; if they break down – physically or mentally?

Remember the old adage that, 'Health is wealth – and tax free.' A more balanced lifestyle will ultimately yield a healthier balance sheet.

Yes, there are times when you need to push on – and push yourself to go that added distance and exert that extra effort. That's what self-starters do. On the other hand is what I call the self-stoppers – those who look for any reason to quit the task at hand, stop what they're doing and give themselves more 'rewards' than they warrant – time for a fourth cup of coffee, a five minute computer game break that gobbles up an hour, idle chit-chat with friends during working hours – sooner or later the day has evaporated. Focus is indeed required for success, but the truly successful business person is also disciplined and knows the difference between valuable re-charging and wasteful procrastination.

We're a long time dead. Make the most of every minute, every hour, every day. Of course, take time for rest and play but there's not a moment to waste. Procrastination is a thief of time.

As an author, there are many times when I simply can't get motivated to write one single word – let alone a sentence, paragraph or chapter. I could waste a lifetime waiting for that mythical 'inspiration.' In reality, 95% of the time, it never comes, until ... I just have to glue my butt to the chair, stare at the blank screen and write on regardless; then edit and re-edit.

You wouldn't be reading this today if I didn't set a goal of X hours or X words per week to work on a manuscript. When struggling with any big project, be honest with yourself and ask whether it's best to take a short break to re-charge, or tough it out. Just make sure you don't cop out.

There are indeed times when we are victims of the law of diminishing returns; when we're too tired or bogged down on a particular issue that we can no longer clearly focus. It becomes pointless to bang our head against a brick wall. That's when it's time to re-charge for a set period of time and return to the task with a refreshed way of looking at things.

That reminds me ... I've been typing since dawn on a sunny Easter holiday; well beyond my four-hour goal for the morning. It's time for an invigorating surf. See you in a bit when I'm re-charged with the energy of the ocean (and possibly a chocolate egg!).

93

Wasting time – wasting life

'Yesterday is a cancelled cheque. Tomorrow is a promissory note. Today is cash in hand. Spend it wisely.'

It's been said before and will be said again: far worse than wasting money or resources is wasting time – the most precious and finite resource that humans possess.

This may seem like a bit of a contradiction to the earlier chapter. Let me be very clear that this doesn't mean we all must be workaholics – as already mentioned, it's essential to engage in enjoyable leisure pursuits that re-charge our own batteries.

Yes, I do feel refreshed after that surf! Heading back to my keyboard, I smiled when I saw a young dude with a t-shirt, emblazoned: 'A wasted weekend is not a weekend wasted!'

We may well question his double meaning of 'wasted' but it's hard to argue that we all need some time out – just as fields need to lie in fallow. It's unquestionable that we all place our own value judgements on what is – or is not – a valuable use of time.

Is it wasted time if a teenager spends four hours on an interactive computer game – or their grandmother plays bridge all afternoon? Is it wasted time to watch a soapie, a documentary or the news on TV? Or read a novel? Is it wasted time to passively watch others play sport when you could do with some exercise yourself? Again, **ID** – **I**t **D**epends. A business executive may unwind over a game of tennis, which clearly wouldn't be a form of relaxation for Roger Federer.

It's not the purpose of this book to judge – just encourage everyone to be more aware of how they actually spend their time at work and play. Admittedly, we all have different definitions of purpose or what is important to us, but continually drifting along with no clear goals or sense of purpose whatsoever is probably a waste of time – and of life.

There are many excellent books on time management and I encourage you to read one or two. It is certainly not a waste of time to do so – don't make the excuse that you don't have time to read a time management book. It is not the purpose of this book to expand on those but from a workplace standpoint, simply consider *every* meeting, *every* phone call, *every* email and *every* process – does it add value or cost to your business, or just waste time?

We talk of 'killing time' when indeed, time eventually kills us all. every moment is precious. We can replace plant and equipment. We can recover lost computer files. We can never recoup lost hours.

It's a good time management principle to have a 'to do' list and I'd be lost without mine. However, sometimes, when the list seems overwhelming, I wonder if I also need to have a ‘stop doing’ list.

Top of that list would be...

94

Meaningless meetings

Admittedly, it may not be possible or practical to eliminate 'politically necessary' or even useless meetings, but at least try to shorten them. State a clearly defined purpose and agenda up front – and stick to it.

Do you need to fly across the country or drive across town for a meeting – or would a phone call or teleconference achieve the same result? Often, there is simply no substitute for the added intangible value we achieve through to face-to-face contact – two heads can be better than one and there is indeed unquestionable value in synergies from brainstorming.

Just consider whether you need two people in the meeting, five or a dozen? It's not often likely the latter and there seems to be an inverse relationship between the number of people present and a successful outcome.

95

Conferences or junkets?

So are conferences are a waste of time and money? They can potentially be a great investment to gather like-minded groups of individuals to share information and team build in a more informal environment, but unless they have a clearly defined focus and theme, they may be little more than a junket.

Here, I must declare a vested interest, as most of my revenue comes from being a keynote speaker.

During the GFC, it was somewhat concerning – but not at all surprising – that many organisations cut back on conferences. I'd have probably done the same when I was responsible for IBM's incentive events, as conferences are usually a discretionary expense. Luckily, for me, business was booming for us in those days and our team had generous budgets to work with. even then, I'd question whether some expenditure was adding value or cost to the conference? Did we really need 150 live elephants at the welcome dinner in Bangkok?

These days, I'd more likely ask:

- Can we hold the event at a lower cost location?
- Is it possible to take advantage of cheaper airfares?
- Would it hurt to book a four-star hotel instead of a five-star one?
- Do we really need lobster on the menu?

- What about the floral arrangement on the table?
- Could a quarterly conference be held twice a year? Or an annual one held bi-annually?

Hesitate before you eliminate meetings and conferences completely. After all, there can sometimes be as much value from what is achieved outside the formal meeting structure, through *informal* interaction with colleagues, customers and suppliers.

96

Networking

Never under estimate the power of networking. It can be worthwhile, but make sure you don't simply attend a multitude of networking forums under the guise of making contacts, rather than focusing on getting on with the job at hand.

Sure, you can combine work with fun. You can socialise and make valuable work contacts at the same time. It's also OK if you just want to have a chat or party.

Just know the difference and think about whether you're using your time wisely at that point in time.

97

Social media – networking or just more work?

There's no question that social networking sites such as Facebook, My Space, Linked In and Twitter, to name a few, are rising in popularity. I've reluctantly signed up for a couple and believe they can be powerful tools for many markets. They provide the medium for customers and stakeholders to no longer just be passive agents in the marketing process. We can now learn as much about a company or product as we wish and can tell others through blogs, podcasts or YouTube. You-tube and You-tell!

Authenticity is key and if you don't live up to your promise, news will spreads like wildfire amongst consumers. The bigger the organisation, the bigger the target for disgruntled bloggers. The whole concept of viral marketing is well beyond the scope of this book but it's worth noting that, historically and statistically, a disgruntled customer used to tell on average 15 other people through word of mouth. now, they can now tell thousands about their bad experience with your product – through word of mouse!

Sites like Google and Wikipedia now make information a commodity, and it's important to sort the wheat from the chaff; to sift knowledge from an information dump; to filter wisdom from amidst that knowledge.

As someone closer to pension age than puberty, I honestly don't know what percentage of my time should be allocated to online networking sites – or whether it's just more work, given my target markets. However, if our markets change, we must do likewise.

But since *The Australian* newspaper reported on August 4, 2009, that Microsoft founder and mega-billionaire Bill Gates closed his Facebook account, because it cost too much time to weed through his 10,000 'friend' requests in the cyber world, I no longer feel obliged to update mine on a regular basis.

98

Wasted worry

Don't waste time worrying about people and events over which you have no control. This is easier said than done.

There are times when we have something that is well worth worrying about – in either our professional and personal lives. However, there are many more hours wasted in worthless worry when we feel overwhelmed by circumstances. That's when we need to focus on just one or two of the most important priorities – and let the rest wait.

I know. I've been there with sleepless nights that rendered me even less productive the next morning; less able to muster my thoughts and actions to focus on practical priorities to reduce stress and worry.

I've wasted enough emotional energy to power the Hoover Dam imagining a conversation that may take place over a conflict that never happens: 'If he says that, then I'll say this...'

My mother was a world class worrier, yet often told me: 'Cross your bridges when you come to them, or you pay the toll twice.'

It's said that we sometimes teach what we need to learn – and believe me, I've got lots to learn about living in the moment. I've read books and listened to meditations. These tools have helped me gradually get a bit better at worrying a bit less. Yet I still catch myself fretting, instead of focusing.

Maybe one day, I'll internalise – not just intellectualise – the wisdom of Mark Twain, who said: 'I am an old man and have known a great many troubles, but most of them never happened.'

99

The best things in life are free

Cost is a four letter word that causes managers to curse at excesses. Value is a five letter word that warrants smiles all around.

Whether faced with boom times or global recession, it's easy to forget that the best things in life are free. A friendly smile costs nothing but adds value to customers who will want to come back.

Many years ago, the owner of a take away shop near my office fully comprehended this concept. Every morning, Eddie greeted me with a smile, a cheery comment and the occasional joke as he squeezed my two dollar glass of orange juice. I'm not a morning person, but he always got my day off to a good start with his cheerfulness.

A competitor opened only a few shops away and sold exactly the same orange juice for $1.80. Over a period of a year, that would be worth $48 to me. It seemed a sensible decision to make the switch.

But I didn't switch. Eddie's friendly smile every day was worth far more than 20 cents a day. The competition raised their prices to his level a few weeks later as they were simply undercutting to get into the market. There's still a queue of people at Eddie's each morning who obviously place a high value on his low cost, positive attitude. Eddie understands the simple formula of treating customers like long-term appreciating assets.

Likewise, a few pleasant words of encouragement can motivate staff to give that little bit extra. Writer Miguel Cruzatta says it best:

'Courtesy is like air in your tyres. It doesn't cost anything but makes travel more pleasant.'

So too, with our own journeys...

Some people will always be all consumed by all things consumable. They know the cost of everything but the value of nothing.

We now see a growing shift from rampant consumerism to individuals who increasingly strive to make their lives worth living as their living is being made.

In an article titled *Living on Less* in Canada's leading magazine (Maclean's Nov.3, 2008 pp 42-48), Colin Campbell and Jason Kirby write:

> 'A new, "frugal future," as some economists have come to call it, seems all but inevitable. "Frugality is now replacing frivolity," declared Merrill Lynch economist David Rosenberg. Households are about to put on a radical diet; debt is a dirty word again, and living within one's means could soon be a fact of life.
>
> 'But even beyond a deep economic recession, there are signs that meaningful social change is brewing. As environmental fears push us from

> Hummers to hybrids, and a younger, tech-savvy generation rebels against the "Bigger is Better" boomer mantra, a long-overdue cultural shift could be in the works, say observers.
>
> 'People are becoming disillusioned with material excesses spawned by the vast run-up of wealth and income,' says David Grusky, a sociologist at Stanford University. And therein lies a potential silver lining. This financial crisis may be the equivalent of Buckley's cold medicine – awful tasting, but good for what ails us financially and spiritually. In fact, a simpler, pared-down and debt-free lifestyle just might make us happier and healthier than we've been in years.'

Who knows if this is trite or truism? One person's or organisation's extravagance may be another's necessity. The old ordinary could become the new normal.

Whatever your circumstance, it will still be worth asking: Does this add value or cost? Value or cost to my business? Value or cost to my life? Value or cost to the lives of others?

The most important things in life *aren't* things. Bear in mind that we all have different value systems and can still choose to do things that may not add value – whether that value is real or perceived. My bookkeeper asked how much was I paid and how many hours did it take to write this book? He then pointed out (as book keepers do) that I didn't even earn a fraction of the minimal wage.

'Aren't you undermining the premise of the book? It cost you a lot of time for very little return.'

Yes, he was technically correct in terms of any tangible or immediate return on investment, as it's always a gamble in terms of what royalties may eventuate from sales. Yet, we all make choices to invest time and energy in pursuits which may not make sense from a bottom line perspective. We just need to make those as *conscious* choices.

Frankly, as an author, there is no greater intrinsic reward than to receive an appreciative letter from a total stranger, indicating that your words have made a difference. Hey, if you've gained profitable ideas, feel free to enclose a cheque representing a percentage of those profits! Just joking but please do email any success stories for possible inclusion in the next book.

100

Summary – time for action

'There are risks and costs to a program of action. But they are far less than the long range costs and risks of comfortable inaction.' – John F Kennedy

The 2008-9 Global Financial Crisis spread around the globe like wildfire through a drought. Many were burned. Were longer lasting lessons learned? Fires are tragic with loss of life – but are sadly sometimes necessary for forest re-growth.

It was tempting to publish this book at the height of the GFC but rather than evoke any knee-jerk, cost-cutting reactions, we preferred to compile a more considered contents of potential longer-term actions that would stand the test of time.

At the time this goes to print, things seem to have settled down (a bit) on the economic front, but could it happen again? Who knows? According to some anonymous philosopher: 'That dollar saved for a rainy day now buys a smaller umbrella.'

Every cloud, including those dark overcast days of the GFC, does indeed have a silver lining. Stormy financial times can trigger re-thinking old strategies for new paradigms; to reassess whether individuals and organisations add value – or simply cost – to each process. Tumultuous times offer the incentive to re-think.

As mentioned at the start, it would be wonderful to concoct a surefire formula to entice every employee in a big organisation to think like a small business owner. Sadly, that's most unlikely.

Happily, there's no need to become a miser – simply save where and when you can so you have more to spend when and where you need to. Adopt a strategy of micro savings for macro value. eliminate waste. Stimulate value.

Paperclips Don't Grow on Trees is by no means a comprehensive list of possible savings but it may get you started on a review of expenses and ways to reduce your costs without reducing value. If you can't see the forest for the trees ... can you, like a skilled gardener, prudently prune expenditure of deadwood now, to grow value longer term? Is it possible to branch out of traditional thought patterns to nurture budding ideas? Hopefully, we've sowed a few seeds of suggestion so you can likewise plant the seeds of savings in your plant or office.

I know this works – if you work at it! Over the years, I've received many letters and emails from clients that say their organisations have increased productivity 30% or saved $400,000 as a result of what I said on stage or what they've read in my books on customer service and managing change. As much as I'd love to take credit, it's not what I've said that's made a big difference. It's what they've heard. More importantly, it's what they've actually ***done*** with what they've heard that made the real difference! It's how they have creatively adapted the ideas I've shared to work best in their own unique situation.

I could possibly write another 100 pages of specific examples – and the publisher could charge twice the price for this book – but would that add value or cost to you, the reader?

Hopefully, you've got the drift of thinking in this short and simple paperclip paperback. We trust there 'paper clip tips' have triggered a few thoughts. now it's up to you to *apply* at least one idea in your organisation. Do it now – not next week or next year, but *today.* There will never be a perfect time to do so. There will always be a bit of uncertainty as to the value of the steps taken – until you actually take them. What are you waiting for? There can't be val_e with u!

To those of you who 'get it', no further explanation is necessary. For those who don't – no further explanation is possible!

Just remember to ask that vital question – at least three times a day with every purchase, with every hiring decision, with every allocation of time or resource in your professional – and personal – life:

Value or cost? Value or cost? Value or cost?

Otherwise, you've just wasted time reading – and we've just wasted paper.

'The poor person is not one without a dollar–

But one without a dream'

CDV

About the author

Catherine DeVrye, MSc is a #1 best-selling author of 7 books, translated into over a dozen languages. The former Australian executive Woman of the Year is neither an economist nor financier-but has worked as an executive with IBM globally for a decade, previously in government and also as CEO of a charity.

For over 15 years she has successfully run a small business: **CDV** Management **C**lients **D**eserve **V**alue. With this breadth of hands-on experience, she speaks to organizations around the world on client service, thriving on change and turning obstacles to opportunities. She's attended short courses at Harvard and lectured at the Melbourne Mt Eliza Business School but believes the best education is common sense.

Catherine abhors waste and adores nature. She resides in an eco friendly home in Sydney and travels more miles on her bicycle than in her fuel-efficient car.

For more about Catherine see: www.greatmotivation.com.

Catherine will welcome your contribution to her next book, *Paperclip Tips.* If used, you'll not only receive an acknowledgement but a free copy of the next book.

For further information on Catherine DeVrye's other books and her availability to customise a presentation for your next conference, please contact:

www.greatmotivation.com, email: office@greatmotivation.com
PO Box 559, Manly, NSW 1655, Australia
Phone 61-2-9977 3177, fax 61-2-99773122

Acknowledgements

'It's amazing how much you can accomplish if you don't care who gets the credit' Harry Truman

It would be remiss of me if I didn't credit those who have contributed to this book in the spirit of a 'paperclip partnership'.

To my many marvelous clients and bureaus who have given me the privilege to speak to their teams and gain a unique insight into the operations of first class organisations around the world.

To Dr Edward De Bono for being an icon of lateral thinking and generously providing comment on the draft of the manuscript; and to Mark Norton for his insights.

To former New Zealand Consul General, Paul Cotton, wherever he may be, for first sharing his paper clip thinking over twenty years ago (I've tried to track him down via Rotary and the New Zealand Consulate in Sydney-but with no luck. So, if any reader has his contact details, please let me know so I can send him a copy of the book with my thanks.

To everyone at Woodslane Publishing: Andrew Swaffer, Antonia Marshall and their teams. And to David Grant of Infinite Ideas in the UK for introducing me to them. It's great to work with a small and flexible team in my local neighborhood to bring this book to the wider world.

To Richard Oldcorn, a friend and financial advisor; for casting an eye over the first draft to save me from being seen in public with the equivalent of fiscally unsound spinach on my teeth. He also provided examples from his advertising days in the UK

To Rachel Yabsley, a delightful young woman who will be a brilliant architect. This baby boomer has appreciated her Gen Y enthusiasm, talent, design and diligence to help out in the office from time to time, throughout her studies.

To Kelly Bourke, Fiona Barry, Liz Burrows, Rosemary Cottrell, Nina Caruso, Harvey Gordon, Gillian Gray, Prakash Idnani, Helen Murrell, Michele Provest, Natalie Raper, John Purdie-Smith, Sue Sacker, Kirsty Spraggon Monika Taus, Candy Tymson and Alan Walker—they offered examples, a sounding board-and most importantly-friendship.

To IBM who unknowingly gave me the foundations to start my own business.

I would also like to acknowledge the Blue Dragon Children's Foundation in Vietnam. When I volunteered in Hanoi, I saw first hand that they didn't waste a cent-and that all donations went directly to help give street kids a new start in life.

A percentage of all sales from this book will go towards helping those amazing individuals who, on a daily basis, add value to the lives of those less fortunate.

Donations are tax deductible and can be made to www.bdcf.org.

blue dragon

CHILDREN'S FOUNDATION

Woodslane Press

Woodslane Press is a growing book publisher based on the Sydney's northern Beaches. For more details of other books and materials by Catherine DeVyre, other business titles published by Woodslane Press, plus titles that Woodslane distributes on behalf of other publishers, see www.woodslane.com.au. All titles are available via you local bookshop, but in case of difficulty can be ordered direct via www.woodslaneon line.com.au or 02-9970-5111.

Titles include:

Good Service is Good Business-7 Simple Strategies for Success By Catherine DeVyre

A #1 best-selling book, filled with practical case studies and examples of how service can boost your bottom line.

The Customer Service Zoo-Create Customers for Life-and a Life for Yourself By Catherine De-Vyre

A parable using animal analogies to simplify and inspire your service delivery

Hot Lemon & Honey: Reflections for Success in Times of Change By Catherine DeVyre

A best-selling book of which Sir Edmund Hillary said: 'information in this book can lead you on the road to success'.

Persuasion & Influence: The Science and Art of Effective Presentation By Bruce Hilliard

The complete guide to making presentations that convince, from audience profiling to setting the structure, scripting to presentation styles.

People Glue: Employee Engagement & Retention Solutions that Stick! By Ian Hutchinson

'Highly recommended, 9 out of 10. Provides a different perspective on employee engagement and practical solutions on how to improve it.'

Back Cover Material

PAPER CLIPS
DON'T GROW ON TREES

The 7 most expensive words
in any organisation are...
'We have always done it that way.'

Running a business is tough in the best of times but when things go well, it's easy to be complacent. Few business owners and leaders are complacent today, however. After decades of growth and prosperity, the 'GFC' was a wake-up call for many, and a reminder that prudent financial business practices not only deliver greater margins but can prove a lifeline in difficult times; as most obstacles present opportunities.

This insightful, easy to read book offers business owners and managers practical, positive options to look at what they can do to **add value** to and reduce the costs of their operation. Short, punchy chapters show how to eliminate waste and stimulate value.

Catherine DeVrye is not an economist, but worked with IBM globally for a decade, the government, and an NGO for a number of years and has successfully run a small business for over 15 years. Catherine is a #1 best-selling author, winner of the Australian Executive Woman of the Year Award and thought leader. She has attended courses at Harvard, lectured at the Melbourne Mt. Eliza Business School and speaks to organisations around the world on client service, thriving on change and turning obstacles to opportunities. She resides in an eco-friendly home in Sydney and cycles to work.

Books For ALL Kinds of Readers

At ReadHowYouWant we understand that one size does not fit all types of readers. Our innovative, patent pending technology allows us to design new formats to make reading easier and more enjoyable for you. This helps improve your speed of reading and your comprehension. Our EasyRead printed books have been optimized to improve word recognition, ease eye tracking by adjusting word and line spacing as well as minimizing hyphenation. Our EasyRead SuperLarge editions have been developed to make reading easier and more accessible for vision-impaired readers. We offer Braille and DAISY formats of our books and all popular E-Book formats.

Made in United States
Orlando, FL
04 November 2026

90202361R00140